A Day in Tuscany

Dario Castagno

A Day in Tuscany

MORE CONFESSIONS
OF A CHIANTI TOUR GUIDE

Betti
EDITRICE

Umor che dalla vite cola

Contents

Contents

To the loving memory of Jonathan Radford

Foreword

After the success of my previous book, *Too Much Tuscan Sun; Confessions of a Chianti Tour Guide*, many people suggested I write a sequel. The idea intrigued me . . . but I'd never really considered myself a writer. The first book had been written just for fun, to help fill my evenings. If someone had told me at the time that it would not only be published but be published successfully, propelling me on a whirlwind of TV appearances, magazine interviews, and a coast-to-coast publicity tour of the United States, I'd have thought they were having me on . . . or just plain nuts.

And yet, bizarrely, so it was: I found myself, a high-school dropout, standing at a podium, lecturing genuine academics. And eventually I thought, *Well . . . if the Swiss can win the America's Cup, and the Jamaicans can have an Olympic bobsled team, then anything is possible. I can go from being someone who wrote a book to being someone who writes books.*

I spent many weeks trying to figure out what I could write about. People who liked the first book asked for more stories of my experiences with tourists, but I had used the best of that material in *Too Much Tuscan Sun*. Others suggested that I just make up some wild stories and pretend they were real, but if experience has taught me anything, it's that the truth is always stranger and more wonderful than anything I could invent from whole cloth.

I received many e-mails from readers asking me to write more about my life in Vagliagli, but to be honest, I thought that the beauty of my existence lay in its utter simplicity. A diary of my everyday life would no doubt strike readers as uneventful.

It took distance, and time, to make me see differently. The day after I returned from my three-month American book tour, something magical occurred. I didn't wake up that morning with the idea of writing a book, but as I wandered my home territory, reconnecting with familiar sights, sounds, aromas, and (especially) friends and neighbors, I began to realize just how rich my life here is. Each new vista and encounter brought back a wealth of anecdote, folklore, history, and just plain gossip that I had taken for granted before my stay in America.

So much happened that day to jar my memory and stir my unconscious mind that I realized I was surrounded by material for a book. In fact, I might as well have been collecting ideas my whole life, without realizing it, for some as-yet-unsuspected purpose.

When I returned home from that memorable first day back in the Chianti hills, I sat down and started writing an account of it. Within a few weeks I had a manuscript ready to send off to my tour client turned friend and book collaborator, Robert Rodi in Chicago, and then to the publisher.

Every event included in this book happened on that early-spring day of 2005. Even the serendipitous lunch incident. You may believe it . . . you may not . . . but whatever you do: *Enjoy!*

Dario Castagno

4:08 A.M.

Maybe it's the jet lag, or maybe just the excitement of having returned to my beloved hills, but I awaken very early. I normally sleep with my shutters open because I like to rise with the first rays of the sun, but right now it's still invincibly dark. I try to go back to sleep but it's useless. I can still hear the monotonous roar of the Boeing 777 echoing in my head. I extend my arm to the empty space beside me; it's been more than a year, but I'm still not used to having the bed all to myself. I turn to face the photo of Cristina that sits on the bedside table and is so vivid in my mind. I'm very fond of this picture: She's crouched down, embracing my late dog Dick Rogers, and I think that here she's at her best—smiling ear-to-ear with a loving expression on her face. I don't understand why she's gone. I continue to leave my keys in the front door in case she returns. How I miss her . . .

I pass an hour or so in drowsy contemplation. Now the sun extends its first tentative rays into the sky like a swimmer testing the water with his toe. All is well, for soon the sun begins to rise from behind the hills, outlining them a majestic red. As the sky brightens and the stars gently vanish, I notice the light blue Samsonite suitcase that I hauled around for months through innumerable airport terminals: It's still waiting to be unpacked. Feeling its silent rebuke, I crawl out of bed.

I make my way down the flight of granite steps and prepare a long brew of *caffè d'orzo* that I sweeten with a teaspoon of honey. I then toast a slice of Tuscan bread, cover it with precious extra-virgin olive oil, add a pinch of salt, and rub a fresh tomato on the crusty surface. I feel like I'm in heaven. For the first time in many weeks, I sit on the terrace with my feet on the brick wall and simply enjoy the spectacle. The sun slowly takes possession of the landscape, flooding with incandescence the castles and villas scattered across the hilltops and valleys.

My village, Vagliagli, is yet fast asleep. The only sounds are the baying of a group of hunting dogs in their kennels, eager to be out and on the scent of wild boar, and the distinctive call of the cuckoo echoing down the valley. The local church bell chimes six o'clock. Its stone tower glows in reflected sun.

Already it's unusually warm. As I prepare to sip from the steaming ceramic cup, I spot in the distance a hot-air balloon floating above the oak trees. In the awed silence of this Chianti morning, it renders the atmosphere, if possible, even more magical. The view suddenly brings back fond memories of my brief association with a delightful local balloon club . . .

The Chianti Balloon Club

Early in my career as a tour guide, I befriended a distinctive Swiss gentleman who owned a stone farmhouse tucked away in the Chianti hills that he had patiently restored with his own hands. I always envied its gorgeous location; I could've happily spent hours on its terrace enjoying the vista, which incorporated both the local countryside and the towers of Siena rising triumphantly into the sky.

Our first meeting took the form of an interview for a local magazine that he often wrote for. Friedrich had come across a brochure publicizing my Rooster Tours, and he saw in me a potential article. He seemed to be intrigued by the services I was offering: accompanying small groups of visitors in a four-wheel drive vehicle to discover the Chianti countryside off the beaten track.

We arranged to meet in a run-down bar in Siena. There I found myself shaking hands with a lanky young man, an outsized cowboy hat hiding his complete baldness, despite what I later discovered to be a flawless skull—perfectly round, no imperfections or lumps. Friedrich had clearly been cultivating and trimming his amazing handlebar mustache with care. He wore a jeans jacket that matched a pair of blue jeans he'd tucked into heavy brown boots. My first thought was: *It's the Red Baron reincarnated!* Curiously, months later, I discovered that he was indeed a baron, even though he preferred keeping this under wraps—unlike so many pompous toffs I'd known who boasted about their blue-blooded origins.

At the end of the interview as we started to relax, our conversation turned to other subjects. Friedrich told me about his passion for flying (*There you go,* I thought to myself, while failing to suppress a giggle, *he* is *the Red Baron!*), and he told me how he'd recently obtained a license to fly hot-air balloons. This had inspired him to found the Chianti Balloon Club, with the intent to organize flights for tourists over the local hills. We'd hit it off sufficiently for him to ask me, now, whether I'd like to join his team.

In those days my Rooster Tours hadn't yet taken off, and if someone had offered me a job shoveling manure in a chicken coop, I'd have accepted. Of course I agreed enthusiastically. He took me to see the beautiful red-and-yellow-striped balloon that he kept in an old barn on his property.

Friedrich's lawn was large enough to accommodate inflating the balloon and was thus perfect for departures. He explained that because hot-air balloons can fly only in the direction of the wind, and that the only control a pilot exercises is the ability to go up or down, he needed a ground crew to follow him during his flights, to pick him up at his landing sites, and then to drive him back to home base. It was fundamental that this person—whom I realized by now would be me—be at the designated spot before landing in order to capture the rope and tether the balloon to the ground. During the flight, he continued, he would keep me constantly updated on his location by walkie-talkie. He would also provide me with his nine-seater Land Rover, to which he'd hooked a trailer large enough to hold the basket and gas burner. In a few minutes we shook hands again, putting the seal on our working partnership—and burgeoning friendship.

We spent the next weeks scattering our promotional brochures among the various hotels in the area. After just ten days Friedrich called me with excitement in his voice to tell me that a German couple had purchased a flight as a birthday surprise for Guenther, and was I available on Wednesday?

"Yes, of course," I said. "Who's Guenther?"

"I have no idea," Friedrich replied. "The important thing is, we've booked our first flight!"

On the designated day I awakened at dawn—Friedrich wanted to take advantage of the more powerful thermal winds of early morning. The stars were still visible in the crystal-clear sky, the wind was low and constant, and there wasn't so much as a cloud on the horizon . . . *A perfect summer morning,* I thought as I closed the shutters and kissed Cristina on her forehead—gently, so as not to pull her from the arms of Morpheus.

The day was cool and the drive pleasant along the deserted roads, and as I approached Friedrich's airfield, the sun emerged from behind Pratomagno Mountain, inundating the valleys with an almost fairy-tale golden glow. My appreciation of such beauty was cut short, however: A large porcupine dashed across the road before me, leaving behind a trail of quills (as they always do when alarmed). I managed to miss the thing by mere inches, and also to miss careering into the ditch. I didn't know what kind of omen this was, but I was young enough not to care too much.

Moments later I reached the house, parked next to Friederich's shed, then set out across the lawn. He was already busy with a couple of helpers, inflating the gigantic sheath with butane gas. After about twenty minutes the balloon was fully inflated and towered over our heads, the ropes firmly tightened to prevent it sailing clean away. I stepped up and greeted Friedrich, who seemed understandably nervous. For this special occasion he was sporting an elegant white jet pilot's shirt festooned with collar badges.

"No sign of clients yet, Dario," he said while glancing at his watch for perhaps the fiftieth time since I'd greeted him.

Just then a black Mercedes entered through the open gate and rolled up the gravel driveway in a cloud of dust. As it drew nearer we recognized a German license plate. Our first Chianti Balloon Club clients had arrived.

A handsome older couple stepped out of the car. At first glance I guessed them to be somewhere in their late sixties. She was dressed head-to-toe in an elegant expensive ensemble, possibly Prada, with a pair of white-framed sunglasses that she politely removed as she shook our hands. He was equally dashing in a yachting jacket and sailor hat. I wondered for a moment at this odd choice of clothing—we were far from the ocean—but then I realized he would soon be, in a sense, sailing.

Herr and Frau Mueller now told us that Guenther hadn't slept a wink all night, so impatient was he for his birthday surprise. Friedrich and I glanced at each other to gauge which of us would be asking the obvious question—but of course I was just a crew member. Friedrich cleared his throat and said, "Well, that's fine. But . . . where *is* the birthday boy?"

The Muellers said, in eerie unison, "Guenther iss in ze car. Ve vill fetch im immediately." With German precision they pivoted on their heels and opened the car's rear door—and to our astonishment a huge Doberman pinscher of rare beauty leapt out, wagging his tail in delight. " Ziss iss Guenther ze Third," Mr. Mueller told us as the canine politely sat and raised a paw, which we felt obliged to shake.

"Vell, are you ready, Guenther, my boy?" Mrs. Mueller said, stroking his head. His tongue lolled out of his mouth as he looked up at her adoringly.

We were at a loss for a moment; we had, after all, no experience whatsoever in escorting clients to the launch site, and our maiden effort was to be made more complex by our first client belonging to an entirely unexpected species. Yet the Muellers seemed oblivious to our perplexity. Not once did they reveal even a hint of awareness that the situation was unusual.

As we led the group to the balloon, Guenther strained against his leash in excitement, and we could see that he wore a big black collar that appeared to be studded with diamonds.

Perhaps they were fake—but then, given the obvious pampering the Muellers lavished on the dog, perhaps they weren't. The closer we got to the balloon, now swaying to and fro in the light morning wind, the more impatient Guenther got. I feared he might actually break the leash.

"Vhen must ve return for Guenther, Herr Friedrich?" Mrs. Mueller asked.

Friedrich actually faltered in his step, he was so surprised. "You—you aren't *coming*?"

"Oh, no, iss Guenther's birthday treat, not ours. Ve vill go for a quick svim and zhen return vhen you say."

Friedrich somehow composed himself long enough to explain that the flight would last approximately three hours, and the drive back to the launch site less than half an hour. The Muellers checked their watches, then joined us for a toast as Friedrich popped open a bottle of champagne to initiate the enterprise.

After giving their pooch a final briefing ("Be a *verrry* goot boy, my Guenther") and a long list of endearments in German, the pair left. When their car pulled away, Friedrich and I were left standing with Guenther at our feet, staring up at us as if to say, *When do we start?*

We were silent for a moment; I had no idea what must be running through Friedrich's mind. But then he surprised me by rolling up his sleeves and barking orders to his other helpers, all business. "Dario, grab the hound and lower him into the basket," he said, turning to me. "Let's get this show on the road."

I knelt before the dog, patted him on the head, looked him in the eye, and, drawing courage from his seemingly friendly expression, said, "Okay, Guenther—you're not going to make things difficult, are you? You'll work with me here, right?" He extended his enormous tongue and slurped my face, leaving me with a sheen of saliva. Then he lay down on his back and extended his legs in the air. I put my right hand under his impressive-looking collar and with my left embraced his backside while I gently raised him up. I kept expecting a snarl of protest, or worse, but he just kept licking me, as though my head were a cone of gelato. I carried him to the basket, where I handed him over to Friedrich, who was now ready to take off. Gingerly he set the dog down. Guenther jumped up and hung his forepaws over the rim. Now *he* was ready for takeoff, too.

We released the ropes, and the balloon rose heavenward. I jumped into the Land Rover and pulled away, keeping one eye on the balloon as it sailed silently into the Chianti sky, floating delicately westward, just above the treetops. It wasn't nearly as easy as I'd imagined to keep the balloon in view, due to the vast acres of unnavigable forest that I had to skirt by whatever roads I could find. Even so, I managed to remain in fairly close range, at least enough to see Guenther's handsome head peering over the basket rim, barking with delight and enjoying every moment of this new experience.

I called Friedrich on the walkie-talkie and asked how things were proceeding up there. He told me that Guenther was behaving well and having a great time, which was confirmed by the staccato *woof-woof-woof*ing that punctuated Friedrich's words. I signed off and was overcome by hilarity. For a moment I even envied the dog, imagining the panorama of Chianti he was enjoying from up there: the vast sweep of the vines now covered in leaves and almost ready to give birth to their ruby-red grapes, the rows of ancient, silvery olive trees, the thick oak forests giving sanctuary to wildlife of all kinds.

And so the hours passed, with the balloon moving majestically across the landscape and me in the Land Rover, giving increasingly jealous chase. I was just wondering whether the castles and villages were as beautiful from a bird's-eye view as they were from the ground when Friedrich interrupted my day-dream by calling to say he'd spotted an open field and would be starting his descent. "Be sure to get there in time to grab the tether," he added.

When I reached the field he'd chosen, I saw at once that it wasn't uncultivated; small green blades of young wheat had just started to pop from the earth. I called Friedrich and tried to warn him, but he'd already gained too much momentum to pull up again. He advised me to invent some suitable explanation in case the farmer appeared.

Of course the farmer appeared—balloons descending in rural Chianti don't go unnoticed. Before I'd had even a moment to find something to say, he came barreling across the field toward me, waving his fists and howling virulent Tuscan oaths (which I'll refrain from translating here). The only thing I could think of was that if we did in fact come to blows, I'd soon have a Doberman on hand to defend me!

When the farmer got closer, I recognized him as Gosto, a big local farmer known as "Bucket" because of the huge quantities of wine he was capable of downing in the local *osterias*. He had other legendary traits as well: He'd lost three fingers cutting wood with a chain saw, and was famous for his repertoire of epithets and foul language—and for being almost pathologically superstitious.

It was this last trait I had in mind when he got close enough to recognize me and screamed, "What the hell do you think you're doing, Dario? Get off my field before I call the *carabinieri*!"

"Gosto!" I retorted as I chased one of the tethers Friedrich had dropped from the basket. "Get over here and grab a rope! Don't you know that if a hot-air balloon lands in your field, you're guaranteed a bumper crop?"

Gosto stopped swearing enough to consider this. He couldn't possibly have heard the legend before, since I'd just made it up, but apparently he didn't want to risk jinxing himself. He calmed down and pitched right in; despite only having two fingers on his right hand he pulled his rope with incredible strength, and thanks to his help the balloon came to a gentle landing, without too much damage to his young wheat. He even entertained Guenther while we packed up the equipment and loaded the basket onto the trailer. All things considered, we decided the least we could do was give him the entire champagne breakfast our clients were meant to enjoy upon landing. (Clearly, Guenther wouldn't miss it.) He emptied the bottle of sparkling wine with a couple of gulps—"Bucket" indeed.

On the way back Friedrich and I rehashed the events of the morning from our separate perspectives, and each time we laughed, Guenther howled in accompaniment from the backseat. On our return we found the Muellers impatiently waiting. Guenther leapt out of the vehicle and bounded toward them, wagging his tail almost lethally. The trio embraced emotionally.

"Guenther has been wonderfully behaved," Friedrich said, "and he enjoyed every moment of the flight."

"Vell zen," said Mrs. Mueller, "you must do us vun more favor." She returned to her car and produced a birthday cake made entirely of dog food, with four big black German sausages stuck in vertically in place of candles. "Ve vill all sing Happy Birthday to Guenther."

After all we'd been through that morning, nothing could

throw us . . . although I did have a bit of trouble keeping a straight face. Afterward our young client devoured the cake in a matter of minutes, while the Muellers again thanked us for having taken care of Guenther the Third.

On his way back to the Mercedes, Guenther left a present for us as well—a big, black steaming one right on Friedrich's driveway. We decided to accept it in the spirit in which it was given.

I helped Friedrich through several more flights before he decided the Chianti Balloon Club wasn't such a good idea after all, and quit. He continues to fly for his own pleasure, though, and it's not uncommon, on a clear summer morning, to see his red-and-yellow folly floating peacefully through the skies.

As for Gosto, that year he enjoyed a very abundant crop, and in the wine bars he let it be known that it had all been thanks to the good luck of a balloon landing in his field.

Today many balloon trips are offered in Tuscany, and the belief that a balloon landing in a cultivated field guarantees a good crop is widely held. I wonder if I was the first to invent the story, or whether it's only the most obvious excuse to come to mind at the sight of an angry farmer running toward you, fists waving in the air.

7:14 A.M.

The sun has now risen fully, and the village is coming to life. The first cars zip past my house, carrying commuters to work in Siena, their swiftness at odds with the leisurely pace of a few strolling retirees. My village of Vagliagli (which translates as "valley of garlic") is a graceful hamlet perched on a beautiful hill on the southern border of the Chianti region. Its origins, as is the case for most of the villages around here, are lost in the mists of time. Etruscan tombs have been dug out close by that prove the area was already settled BC, and later it became a Roman colony. During the Middle Ages the settlement was probably fortified and used as an outpost during the endless wars between Siena and Florence. At the end of the battles in the sixteenth century, the imposing walls and towers gradually were taken down and Vagliagli transformed into a peaceful village. Today there are no more than three hundred souls, the majority of which work for three major wineries that own the vineyards surrounding the village. A minority commutes 15 miles southwards on a spectacular twisty panoramic road that winds through a scenery of vineyards, olive groves, and thick oak forests to work in the banks and hospital in Siena. Still today this remains the only paved road leading to the village; the other accesses coming from north, east, and west are gravel. For this reason Vagliagli has remained a bit cut off from the busy world and outside of the main tourist tracks. The village center is built around a rectangular square with a little bar, a grocery store, a post office (that will be closing soon), a pharmacy that opens three days a week, a well-known restaurant, and a wine bar that opens only for dinner. As I take in the movements of the morning, my eye settles on tall Gino, marching proudly as ever up the walk; he definitely doesn't look his age, and has always impressed me with his wonderfully confident sense of style. Even for a morning walk, he's sporting an elegant suit and tie, and his closet must boast a sizable collection of hats—every other day he's tucked his head into a new one. Gino was a prisoner of war in Africa, but despite my many attempts to draw his story from him, he remains resolutely silent on the subject—"for political reasons," he says. This past September, during the village grape fest, I'd stooped to repeatedly refilling his glass of wine, hoping inebriation would loosen his lips, with the result that he drank me under the table and walked away none the worse for wear. (I wish I could say the same for myself.)

Behind him, his step much slower and bent forward on his stick, is Raffaele, whom I know won't go very far; it's his habit to take possession of the first wooden bench overlooking the valley like a king on a throne. Since he stopped smoking he's taken to carrying a vine twig in his inner pocket, which he'll stick into the corner of his mouth.

Now come the kids, bursting out of their homes and heading for school, their young shoulders easily bearing backpacks groaning with battered books. As they file noisily into the yellow school bus, some of them wave to me from the windows. I raise my cup to them, and instantly a chorus of "*Ciao, Inglese*" echoes from the back of my mind. I shut my eyes and recall those sweet days . . .

Ciao, Inglese

When I was nine years old, my parents decided to leave London and return to Italy. On a winter morning my father crammed the Volvo with luggage and the four of us, my parents, brother, and me, plus Suzie the cat, left behind Leopold Road, Wimbledon, and with it our English life and many memories.

After what seemed to me an endless drive through France, we crossed the Alps and entered Italy. We soon reached the Tuscan house my parents had rented temporarily, until they found something suitable to purchase in the area. This stopgap house was on the border of southern Chianti, perched on a hill overlooking the Val d'Elsa. It was part of a fairly large old estate called Caligiano, which comprised a *villa padronale* (manor house) and a series of farmhouses attached to the main structure. The other folks living on the premises were the owners and their tenant farmers, who earned their living cultivating the surrounding fields.

The very first morning I was awakened by the sound of the cock crowing, definitely a new experience for me; up to then my wake-up call had been the annoying jangle of an alarm clock. I opened the shutters and was virtually assaulted by the early-morning sun. Below my window a group of hens and chickens were busily scratching about in search of worms, some of them trailed by their little yellow chicks, while close by on a dry-brick wall stood the rooster, majestically puffing his lungs before releasing his primeval cry. His declaration of supremacy completed, he lowered his crested head toward the coop and patrolled the harem, as though daring anyone now to come and lay claim to them.

As I watched, Suzie cautiously crawled outside for her first escapade on her new turf. Even for her, all these changes must have seemed disorienting. She had, after all, lived her life prowling the rooftops of Victorian-era homes in urban London; now she had to take entirely new bearings, exploring the surrounding wheat fields and vineyards. I wondered, if she'd had a choice, what her preference would have been. My speculations were suddenly interrupted by a violent stirring below: The hens had noticed Suzie. They were darting about, puffed up and flapping their wings to send their chicks to safety. They then organized themselves into an almost military formation around the terrorized invader; Suzie crouched lower and lower to the ground, sensible to the growing threat.

Heads bobbing menacingly, the fowl advanced. Suzie was soon cornered against the stone wall. She managed to escape imminent harm with a great feline leap right over the birds' lines; when she landed she wasted no time in darting up the stairs in disgrace. It must have appalled her that her long nights of literal catfighting with her feline rivals on London rooftops hadn't adequately prepared her for a confrontation with a bevy of birds.

After breakfast I went into the yard to kick my soccer ball about, but I soon had to give up; it had become covered in poultry droppings, and when I trapped it on my chest and then went for a header, I covered myself in chicken shit, too.

I took a quick shower, and then my older brother Cristiano

and I investigated the barn, stacked high with bales of hay. In no time we'd figured out what fun it was to climb to the top and then dive down into their midst, raising vortexes of yellow dust that spun madly in the rays of sun filtering through the narrow vertical window.

After we tired of the game, we decided to explore the property in full. Our first discovery was a small pond full of croaking frogs bordered by soft green moss. Leaning against the adjacent wall was a long wooden pole; an old German military helmet was strapped to it to serve as a bucket. We dipped the pole beneath the pond's surface, and when we fished it out we were delighted to see that we'd actually made a catch: There was a beautiful triton swimming around the rusty helmet. We observed the gorgeous little amphibian for a while, utterly fascinated, before carefully returning it to its habitat and continuing our exploration.

We descended into a vineyard that bordered an oak forest, from which every now and then we heard the unmistakable sounds of a hunt: rifle reports, shouts of encouragement, and the barking of hounds that were no doubt tracking down hares and pheasants. We continued our descent until we reached a river, deep and swift. After stumbling across an old arched stone bridge, we found, on the other side, a set of railway tracks. These we followed for a few miles till we heard the whistle of an approaching engine. My brother produced a small coin from his inner pocket and placed it on one of the rails, and we jumped into a ditch to avoid being hit. When the train passed and we emerged, we checked out the coin; it had been completely flattened and resembled an ancient medallion.

We continued our trek. Soon, behind a curve, we spotted a small brick shed with an old wooden door painted green. The door was unlocked, so we entered. The place was full of tools and wine flasks, and in the corner there was a pile of magazines. We picked one up and leafed through it; it was hard-core pornography. I had never seen anything like it and had a hard time understanding what all those naked people were doing lying on top of each other. Cristiano grinned and patiently explained the mechanics of it all to me, but just when it was getting interesting, we were interrupted by the appearance of an extremely angry man.

He was obviously an employee of the Italian national rail, with the scruffy gray uniform and hat with black plastic peak to prove it. His face was frighteningly red, and when he started shouting at us, we were almost floored by the wallop of his alcoholic breath. Given his bloodshot eyes and the vein on his forehead that looked ready to burst, we dropped the magazines and shot out the door, knocking him to the floor in our haste. He flailed us as he tumbled, but was fortunately far too drunk to catch either of us.

All the same, he scrabbled back to his feet and started chasing us, shouting a stream of profanity. Propelled by fear, we ran heedless of where we were going as long as it was away from him. By great good fortune we soon came to the stone bridge, which we flew across, back to the steep vineyard. Instinctively we began to climb, perhaps sensing that our drunken pursuer would be unlikely to follow, even though this meant returning a different way than we had originally come. But to our horror the railway man, despite the hill's steepness, was still in dogged pursuit.

Cristiano pointed out a small ingress someone had dug into the side of the hill, partially covered by black ivy. Without a word he dived toward it. I followed, my heart now pounding so loudly I could barely hear the shrieks of the man behind us. We pushed the trails of ivy aside and crawled into what seemed to be a long tunnel. The walls were covered with cockroaches, and as we made our way deeper the light disappeared utterly. We were in total darkness. But at least we were safe!

As our joy over escaping the railway man ebbed, it was replaced by growing alarm at being stuck underground in a cockroach-infested tunnel that led nowhere we knew, and which was too narrow to allow us to turn around. Fortunately, the darkness soon began to abate, and to our relief we could soon see a dim light in the distance. Our harrowing escape was now officially a success.

But the surprises weren't over. As we emerged blinking into the bright Tuscan sunlight, we realized that we were right back at Caligiano, our new home. The tunnel, we later learned, had been excavated by a previous generation of farmers as a World War II bomb shelter.

At that moment our mother leaned out the window and shouted "*È pronto!*"—lunch is ready! This was wonderful news, because we were ravenous after all our adventures. But as I approached the house, I noticed that I'd picked up a passenger in the tunnel: A tiny bat, sound asleep, hung head-down from my collar. I gently detached his furry little feet and spent a few minutes observing the bizarre little creature, deep in slumber and unaware of my scrutiny. I turned back and replaced it delicately in the cave, then raced to the house.

When our mother asked what we had done that morning, we shrugged. "*Niente.*" Nothing.

That night, as I lay in bed staring at the wooden beams above my head, I thought about my first day in Italy. Certainly I'd had a great time exploring the surrounding area, and England was already beginning to seem a distant memory. But I was apprehensive all the same, because the next day would be my first at an Italian school. I wasn't worried about the language; at home we'd always spoken Italian and I was almost fluent, though I had a strong British accent (it would later disappear after just a few months). No, my worry was: Would I like it? Would I fit in? . . .

I could hear the sound of a woodworm coming from one of the beams, and I tried to work out the problem in my head: *If a worm eats X inches of the beam every day and the beam is Y feet long, how much time will it take him to devour it all?* I was never good at equations, and within minutes I had bored myself to sleep.

The next day my parents drove us to the local village of Staggia Senese, which in those years had fewer than a thousand inhabitants, and dropped us off at the public school. A bunch of kids were noisily fooling around in front as they waited for the bell marking the beginning of class. My brother and I separated, gravitating toward the students who were more visibly our respective ages. As I approached my peers, several broke away to meet me halfway. They began peppering me with questions: "Where do you live?" "Where are you from?" When I told them I had just moved from London, I instantly became a major attraction. The children pointed at me and called out to the others, "*Inglese, Inglese!*" In those days, some thirty years ago, tourism had not yet taken off; most of my new classmates had never seen a foreigner. Before I knew it I was surrounded by curious eyes and hands, as if I were an alien from outer space who might disappear at any moment.

The bell finally sounded. Luciano, one of my new companions, accompanied me to the classroom and indicated an empty desk I could occupy. The room was full of screaming students, who at the sight of me all came running up, smiling and crying *"Benvenuto, Inglese!"* At the head of the class was a strapping young man with wide shoulders and a thick black mustache; he approached me now with his hand extended. I was surprised to see that he had no authority whatsoever over the students, some of whom were jumping on the desks, others chasing one another and knocking over chairs.

"Benvenuto, Inglese," he said.

"But, I'm not English, *signore*," I protested. "I'm Italian. I just lived in London." To my amazement, the students all roared with laughter, and I wondered if my accent or grammar were really that much poorer than I'd thought; but the mustached man grabbed me with his thick arms and squeezed me affectionately, then put me on his shoulders and marched me around the class, chanting, *"L'Inglese mi ha dato del Signore!* The *Inglese* called me *signore*!" to more roars of laughter from the kids. I was very embarrassed, and not entirely certain what I'd done wrong. Only days before, I'd been at a Jesuit school in London, wearing an uncomfortably starched school uniform and adhering to a rigid structure in which everything had to be done in religious silence to avoid punishment. Now here I was sitting on the teacher's shoulder, with a howling crowd of kids in blue jeans acclaiming me like a teen celebrity. There were even *girls* in the class!

The noise suddenly subsided when an attractive middle-aged blond woman entered and barked, "Mauro, put the poor boy down and go to your desk!" The mustached young man obeyed, and to my astonishment took a seat at the far end of the classroom. So he apparently wasn't the teacher—but then what was this grown man doing here? Was it possible he was a pupil? . . . I couldn't comprehend any of this madness.

The *professoressa* greeted me kindly and told me how happy she was to have an English pupil in her class, and once again I explained that I wasn't English but 100 percent Italian. She looked amused by this, as though I'd insisted I could fly or make time stand still. She then made me sit at her desk and read out loud from her textbook—for the irony was that my first-ever lesson in an Italian school was an hour of English.

After that we had an hour of math, followed by a ten-minute break. I was again cornered and bombarded by questions. "*Inglese*, do people in England really wear bowler hats?" "*Inglese*, is it true that in England everyone takes tea at four o'clock?" "*Inglese*, do the English really eat bacon first thing in the morning?" "*Inglese*, is it true London is always under a fog?" "*Inglese*, do the Scots really wear kilts?" Fortunately the bell saved me yet again.

The rest of the morning passed rapidly and uneventfully, though I was surprised at how strongly the lessons contrasted with what I'd grown used to at Wimbledon College. Here the teachers had a relaxed relationship with their pupils; they were patient with us and extremely cordial, even sweet-natured, a significant difference from the austere British teachers who had bullied us and inflicted corporal punishment for the most trifling of reasons.

At one thirty the lessons ended, and my brother and I met outside to compare notes. I was relieved to hear that his experiences had been similar to mine. We took the school bus home, which was an experience in itself: Before dropping us back at Caligiano, it deposited other kids at farmhouses scattered far and wide around the countryside. Some of the houses seemed to me almost impossibly remote.

One of the other passengers was Mauro, my mustached classmate whom I'd mistaken for the teacher, and who had, I noted, spent most of the day gluing football cards to his scrapbook, completely ignoring the lessons. He was so large that he could scarcely sit in the bus seats, which had been designed for children half his size. All the way to his family's farmhouse he told jokes and stories and kept everyone laughing. I was so curious that I had to ask him why he was in school with us. Taking no offense, he explained that he was the son of a family of sharecroppers, and that once he finished middle school—which in Italy is obligatory—his parents intended to send him to plow the fields at the farm. He had no desire to do any such thing, so he purposely got low marks, forcing the teachers to hold him back, in effect keeping him in middle school indefinitely. Thus far his plan was working beautifully: Since his first year of elementary school he'd succeeded in doing each year twice. At sixteen he was in a class of nine- and ten-year-olds.

To make things even more ridiculous, he looked several years older than his real age—not many sixteen-year-olds grow so tall, or can manage so luxurious a mustache. Despite this—or perhaps because of it—everyone seemed to love him; he was very popular and amusing and lots of fun to play with.

After lunch at home, my brother and I sat down to do our first Italian homework. But we were soon interrupted by a chorus of "*Inglesi, Inglesi,*" from outside. We leaned out the window and were stunned to see that about thirty kids from the local village who had walked the 5 miles to Caligiano to visit us. They'd brought fruit juice and biscuits, and my mother had difficulty fitting them all in the living room. It was great fun, but there was a hint of awkwardness—as though we were somehow disappointing them in being so thoroughly Italian. They gave the impression that they had come all this way expecting to find something exotic.

Before they left, each boy asked my mom if he could have us for lunch after school, and she consented. So for the next several weeks, I found myself every day eating at some different classmate's house. I remember these lunches as very abundant and quickly learned never to leave my plate completely empty or it would immediately be refilled. Each meal was a seemingly endless five-course affair; I often felt as if I would burst. Also, it was normal to be served a glass of red wine—even, in some homes, to be offered a cigarette after the meal.

The parents were as friendly as their children, and despite my continued insistence that I was in fact Italian they preferred to call me *Inglese,* so in the end I gave up. Similarly, at the home of a very tall boy, his mother took one look at me and pronounced that I was short because in England all the people were short. Another time, at the home of a shorter friend, his *mamma* grabbed both my cheeks, squeezed them with all her might, kissed me on my forehead, and remarked that I was very tall . . . but this was normal because all the English were tall.

I will always treasure the memories of that period of my life—my first Tuscan spring, during which my new friends transformed me into a true *chiantigiano.* They taught me where to find wild asparagus, where to steal the plumpest cherries off the trees (and how to avoid getting caught by the farmers), the best rivers for swimming, how to catch trout, and how to distinguish poisonous snakes from the harmless ones—these among many, many other lessons. I remember running through the fields of endless red poppies, playing hide-and-seek in a forest of giant sunflowers, all of it beneath the intensely blue Tuscan skies. It was there I got to know girls for the first time, and became aware of how I would blush and how my heart would race whenever some of them came near me, a phenomenon I had never experienced before. I joined the local soccer team and soon was made captain; and whenever we played, the entire village would flock to see the *Inglese*. A group of girls even wrote a song in my honor that they would sing from the stands each time I scored.

When I turned ten the following year, we moved, as my parents had finally found a house they liked some distance away in Castellina in Chianti. But that brief period in Staggia will remain one of best of my life.

Today Staggia is very different, perhaps ten times the size it was thirty years ago, and it has lost much of its charm and innocence. A foreigner attending the local school today would make no news—many immigrants have flocked to Tuscany in the past decade. Despite this, and the many years that have passed since my arrival there, on the rare occasions that I happen to stop in town, some of my old companions will recognize me and shout out, "*Ciao, Inglese!*"

8:03 A.M.

I finish my cup of *orzo* and decide it's time to face the ordeal of unpacking. First, though, I want to check out the back garden, to see how it has endured the cold winter weeks I've been away.

The rosebush and the jasmine are blooming, and the digitalis, lavender, and rosemary look fine and healthy, though the rosemary needs to be cut back where the heavy snow of February bent its branches. Unfortunately, the sage I planted in the fall needs to be replaced entirely.

The empty terra-cotta pots are virtually crying out for fresh flowers. I decide to fill them this year with pink petunias. I catch sight of an enormous cricket busily devouring one of my cabbage leaves, but given the passion with which it is enjoying the meal and its total indifference to my presence, I decide not to disturb it.

It strikes me anew how clean the air is here; breathing it in makes me feel heady, and reminds me how much I've missed my hills all this time. Deciding that the suitcase can wait awhile longer, I duck back inside and slip on a pair of boots. As I head out the door, I reflexively slip my cell phone in my pocket. But I catch myself and toss it on the couch. Today I can go without.

A back road leads to the top of a hill outside my house. There the wild fennel is releasing its unmistakable licorice scent into the air. I rip one of the refreshing stalks from the ground and place it between my lips.

The path leads to an austere gray granite building called *Astreo*, around whose tower dozens of noisy swallows are joyfully swooping and carousing. Francesco, the young owner of the villa, is leaning out a window enjoying the view, his long hair dancing in the breeze. "Dario," he exclaims, "you're back! Come in, I want to know all about your trip."

I enter through the large wrought-iron gate. While I wait for Francesco to come and greet me, I take in the splendid view from the back garden. Francesco appears and welcomes me warmly, then says, "My mother would be happy to see you. Why not come in for a glass of wine?" I'm thrilled by the invitation: Rosanna Bonelli Flamini is a legend in these hills, the only woman who has ever raced in the Palio of Siena, the famous bareback horse race held every year whose heroes are this area's greatest celebrities . . .

La Ragazza del Palio

We enter the expansive villa and find Rosanna in the living room with her older sister, Rilli, bent over some crosswords. The room is as I remember it: very large, the furniture ancient, the walls covered with photos and portraits of family past and present. Rosanna and Rilli both get up and give me a warm welcome, asking me eagerly how my trip went. Had I really been to New York?

"Twice," I reply, sinking into the couch. As Francesco pulls a cork from one of his homemade bottles of wine and pours us each of us a glass, I tell them about my long walks around the city, venturing on foot from uptown to downtown, and then out of Manhattan to the Bronx and Queens.

There's a moment of silence; Rosanna lights a cigarette, deep in thought. This kind of journey, for most Tuscans—as, indeed, for me before I undertook it—is so exotic as to be unimaginable.

I take advantage of their hospitality and try to draw them out—to get them to answer my stories with ones of their own, which I have always wanted to hear. Luck is with me this day. Before long they're spinning tales with so much intensity and enthusiasm that I ask for a pen and paper, and commence taking notes—though it's difficult to follow because both sisters are speaking at once, fervently enough that they don't realize they're overlapping.

I politely nod from one to the other, encouraging them; but they soon seem almost to forget I'm there, so rapt are they in their reminiscences—and by their very verbal disagreements when the memory of one doesn't accord with the other.

Francesco, seated next to me, acts as moderator and brings them to some order. It's a job he's well suited for, because he knows well the many ways in which Rosanna and Rilli are different—and the ways in which they are startlingly alike. Rilli gives off an aristocratic aura. As usual she's impeccably dressed, modest and elegant, with her black hair drawn back into a neat ponytail. What jewelry she wears is simple but in exquisite taste. She is beyond doubt the more urbane of the two, and in fact lives in the family house on one of the most desirable streets in the center of Siena. Rosanna, the younger sister, is more of a country matron, more casual in her manner and dress, her hair still worn loosely. I imagine that she was quite a tomboy as a girl. No one meeting them for the first time would take them for sisters, but as they like to point out, their differences complement each other, which is why they continue to get on so well. What they have in common, especially as they grow older, is widowhood, an immense love of family—and a pride in their heritage that comes across forcefully as they speak.

The house we're in is a relatively recent edifice. As we sit and talk, the sisters remind me that it was built in 1909 by their grandfather Alessandro Bonelli, who also owned an estate less than a mile away comprised of twelve working farms. For some reason he decided to sell the entire parcel for 65,000 lire (about $30 in U.S. currency around the turn of the nineteenth century) and build this magnificent villa in his favorite spot, here atop the hill. Because of its exposure he named the structure Villa Astreo—Astreo being the mythological father of the four winds. When digging for the foundations began, the workers discovered a granite quarry. Huge chunks were extracted and patiently carved into bricks by the stonemasons living in the village, which were used to construct the villa itself. The construction was completed for a total cost of 81,000 lire, and afterward it was used as a summer retreat by the family. In the 1970s Rosanna decided to move here permanently, along with her two children Francesco and Chiara, and recently they have transformed it into a bed-and-breakfast.

Rilli says that as soon as he sold the estate lands, her grandfather Alessandro had been offered Giannutri—one of the splendid islands of the Tuscan archipelago—for 12,000 lire, but their grandmother Anna didn't like the idea of having to take a boat to go home, and on her behalf Alessandro declined the offer. I look at them incredulously, unable to believe that in those years you could purchase an entire island for such a ridiculous sum. The sisters both sigh at the thought that they might have been the owners of one of the gems of the Mediterranean.

All the same, Francesco adds, the villa was always lucky. In World War II, for instance, it was used by the German army as their headquarters, but was spared Allied bombardment simply because it wasn't on any of the maps.

Rosanna tops up my glass, takes a cigarette from the packet on the marble coffee table, and lights it. The room has a high ceiling and some large windows that open toward the valley. My eyes are again drawn to the family photos, and I notice that among the many faces is that of a very handsome man with dark hair and an easy, open expression. I soon learn that this is Rosanna's and Rilli's father, and Francesco's grandfather, Luigi Bonelli, a famous composer and writer who even had a square named after him in Siena. He composed many memorable operettas, including *Rompicollo* (Daredevil). It's the story of a young girl who races the Palio and ends up winning it for her *contrada*, the *Selva* (Forest). It is of course fiction, inspired by a female jockey named Virginia who—legend holds, perhaps apocryphally—raced in the Palio of 1581.

Rilli, who is eleven years older than Rosanna, says that as a little girl her sister showed an astonishing range of talents: She played the piano, was a gifted painter, and excelled in equestrian sports.

The family, she reminds me, has always been of the *Selva contrada*, their ancestral house having been located in that district; they remain active members and generous donors. I grow excited, as we seem, circuitously, to be closing in on the tale I long most to hear. I refill my glass and this time accept a cigarette from Rosanna. Smoke now suspends from the ceiling down to our heads, giving a kind of mystical air to the room and its ancient wooden furniture.

"In 1957," Rosanna says, delving at last into the story that has made her a local legend, "a famous film director, Zampa, came to town to shoot a movie based on the Palio. The stars were the blond British actress Diana Dors and the great Italian actor Vittorio Gassman, who was then just at the beginning of his career. The movie was about a beautiful young woman staying in Siena who, after an incredible series of circumstances, ends up racing the Palio for the *Chiocciola* [Snail] district—and winning!"

"Just like in *Rompicollo!*" I exclaim.

Rosanna nods. "The director hired four actual Palio jockeys for the film, and one of them was Ganascia, whom I used to hang out with. One morning while filming, Zampa called for the jockeys to prepare them for a particular scene, but only three of them were on the site—the fourth, we discovered later, was completely drunk in a local *osteria*. When word got around, I saw this as my big chance. I implored Ganascia to let me take the role; in costume I would look just like the others, and because I was an accomplished horsewoman, it would be no trouble at all for me to race around the Piazza del campo. Ganascia thought I was pulling his leg; when he realized I was serious he told me I was crazy. But the director was getting impatient, Ganascia finally gave in. He hid my long hair under the helmet and I donned the jockey's suit—no, Dario, I won't tell you which *contrada's* colors I wore. I diligently followed all the instructions the director gave us. It was a thrill to be riding on the *campo*, as though in an actual Palio!

"At the end of filming, we rode toward the town hall and my helmet fell off, revealing my long hair and betraying my sex.

Zampa was furious; he came at me shouting that I was crazy and reckless. I wasn't insured, and what if I had gotten hurt? He would have been in big trouble. I ran home completely unfazed, as I had satisfied my dream of riding bareback around the Piazza del Campo.

"The following day someone knocked on our front door; the filmmakers were looking for me. Thinking they had come to scold me again, I hid in my bedroom. But to my surprise, they had come to inform me that Diana Dors's double had been injured. Seeing no alternative, Zampa had sent them to go find 'the crazy girl' as a replacement. They had me sign a contract, and that same day I found myself at work again in the movie—this time for pay! I was only twenty at the time, and working beside those celebrities was an incredible experience."

We'e all fallen silent listening to Rosanna, even Chiara, who had entered quietly and slipped onto the couch to hear her mother's story. Rosanna lights another cigarette and continues. "But the surprises weren't over—in fact, the biggest one was to come. The filmmaker came up with the wild idea of having me participate in the actual Palio. After all, the story of the film was about a girl jockey riding the race—so what better promotion than a *real* girl jockey doing just that? My *contrada*, alas, had no intention of giving me such an opportunity, and I was very offended. To make matters even more difficult, my father had died a few years before, and my uncle Berto was looking after us. Feeling responsible for me, he made the rounds of every *contrada*, saying his niece was crazy and making sure I received no offers.

"But this is where my father's influence came in. He obviously wanted his daughter to be like his famous Rompicollo, and so he intervened from above. Just a few hours later, the *Aquila* [Eagle] *contrada* made a deal with the film company. They had won the Palio the previous year, and had spent so much on their victory that they were strapped for cash. So they arranged to allow me to ride for a big fee, provided that I myself rode for free. I swear I got absolutely nothing," Rosanna insists, gesticulating passionately, "but this didn't matter, I would have paid *them* to get this opportunity. Still, even today, very few people believe me."

Rilli now passes me a stack of photos of her sister suited up in the Eagle colors; she's quite beautiful, and judging by the gleam in her eyes, I believe she *wasn't* interested in money. Francesco and Chiara apparently think so, too; they're lovingly attuned to their mother's story as though hearing it for the first time.

"I was so thankful to Masoni, the *Aquila* [Eagle] captain, and to all the members of the *contrada,*" Rosanna continues. "On the nights preceding the race, the Eagle boys would come below my window and sing me sweet serenades. In fact, everyone was so wonderful to me that some days after the race, I listened to my heart and did something that normally isn't done in Siena."

A sudden, awkward chill fills the room. "What did you do, Rosanna?" I ask.

"I decided," she says in a low voice, "to become a member of the *Aquila*. And I baptized both Francesco and Chiara in the *contrada* when they were born, years later."

Rilli scowls slightly, as if trying to tell me that her sister has betrayed the family tradition.

"But what about the race itself?" I ask to clear the tension from the air.

"Three days before, at the *tratta* [horse assignment]," Rosanna says, "the *Aquila* drew a horse named Percina. It was her first Palio, but she was fit and strong and I was sure she was suited for the event. There was no need to ask what race name

I wanted to adopt; it had to be Rompicollo, so that I could bring my father's operetta to life.

"The big day arrived. Suddenly I found myself entering the *campo* with the other jockeys. I had thousands of eyes on me, but I was calm and didn't feel the pressure. It was hard to believe, though, that I was about to run one of the most famous and dangerous races in the world.

"The captain had told me not to accept any bribes, just to race the three laps with honor, and that's exactly what I intended to do. Already the race had lost one entrant, as the *Tartuca* [Turtle] *contrada* had to pull out because their horse had been injured that morning. But the competition that remained was impressive.

"I remember the lineup exactly. The *Lupa* [She-wolf], with the jockey Romanino on Archetta, was in first place, then the *Oca* [Goose] with Biba on Ravi. Then me, followed by the *Nicchio* [Shell] with Vittorino on Belfiore, the *Selva* [Forest] with Raffica on Falchetto. The *Leocorno* [Unicorn] had il Terribile [The Terrible]on Gaudenzia. After that, the *Torre* [Tower] with Tristezza [Sadness] on Tanaquilla and the *Drago* [Dragon] with Bazza [Big Chin] on Capriola. And finally the *Civetta* [Owl], with Giove [Jupiter] on Marta. As we took our places, none of the jockeys spoke, and when I timidly pointed out to Vittorino that he was in my place he totally ignored me.

"When the race finally began, everything went so fast. I had a terrible start and was running last; then after the first, perilous turn of San Martino I gained confidence and started to overtake the others. Halfway through the race I was in fourth place and about ready to tackle third, but when I tried to pass the *Lupa*, I took the turn too sharply. I hit my knee on one of the marble columns and fell against the mattresses.

"My race was over. I had agreed that if I fell without hurting myself, I would give a thumbs-up to my sister, who was following the race anxiously from one of the windows. I did this, despite the sudden confusion all around me; the people of the *Torre* accused me of having obstructed their jockey, Tristezza, and a couple even started giving me knocks on my helmet. I was taken away by some rescuers and ushered into the town hall, where I was greeted by many *Aquila* members bearing bunches of flowers. But some furious members of the *Torre* had followed me—chased me, really. I ended up having to flee. The Eagle members used their flowers to try to defend me." Rosanna smiles as she relates this. "I appreciated this attention; maybe I even enjoyed it a little. I didn't want to receive any special courtesies because I was a woman, I wanted to be treated just like all the other jockeys, and as you know, the post-race scuffles are a tradition every jockey must face. Except of course for the winner. In this race, that was Vittorino, who had taken my place in line.

"I decided to stay home a few days, till the boiling spirits had simmered down a bit. Then one morning the maid came to my room and said, 'The Savelli brothers are here to see you,' and I thought, *Oh my God, these two men of the Tower have come to beat me up again.* They owned a butcher shop, these brothers, which didn't make them any less frightening. So as you can imagine I received the news with a certain apprehension.

"When I went downstairs I found them standing in the middle of the hall, a bit red in the face. After an embarrassing silence one of them blurted out, 'The captain of the Tower, Signora Marchesa Pace Misciattelli, sent us to ask your pardon.' Then they gave me a bouquet of flowers and without another word slipped out the door and were gone, like a couple of schoolboys who'd just been punished for a prank. And that was that—I had no more trouble from the *Torre*.

"As for my horse, Percina, unfortunately during the fall she was slightly injured and was no longer able to race, but I am positive that she could have won a Palio.

"Anyway, I became a celebrity. I was on the front page of a very popular weekly magazine, and I got a lot of attention from the press even after that." Rosanna produces the actual magazine, which is atop an article that announces her wedding to her beloved husband. There are other clippings, but before I can examine them Rosanna has me up and off the couch; she takes me to see the original outfit she wore on August 16, 1957, now religiously preserved in a glass case in the living room.

"You know," she says, returning again to her memories, "for over thirty years every time I met Tristezza, the *Torre* jockey, he would say to me, 'Rosanna, you really did me wrong. If you hadn't interfered with me I would have won that Palio.' I always gave him tit for tat—I never lost my pluck—and when I'd finished teasing him back he'd give me a long, amused stare. He chose his name well—*Tristezza*, sadness. Those were the only times I ever saw him smile."

Before we part company, the family shows me some of the guest rooms in their splendid bed-and-breakfast. Then Chiara drives her aunt Rilli back home to Siena, and I find myself on the doorstep with Rosanna. I ask her one final question: "Do you think you could have won the race that day, like your father's Rompicollo?"

There's not even a pause: "*Certo, Dario,*" she replies with a brilliant smile—the same one I saw in the newspaper cutting of 1957; the smile of a twenty-year-old girl, *la ragazza del Palio,* the incarnation of her father's operetta.

I leave the house, thanking Rosanna for her hospitality and

for the delightful early-morning spring conversation . . . but what I'll cherish most of all are those few unguarded moments reliving a local legend.

9:49 A.M.

As I leave the Astreo behind, I admire the irises bordering the sidewalk; they tower over the wild fennel, ranging in color from brilliant violet to shady purple. Moving on, I pass beneath an acacia tree and find dangling among its branches—with no apparent support, as though actually hovering in thin air—a tiny caterpillar. I stop to watch it lower itself along its near-invisible silk line all the way to the ground, swaying gently in the light breeze as it descends.

It's a strange coincidence: Mere minutes after listening rapturously while Rosanna recounted her unique Palio experience, I find the very creature that symbolizes my own district, the Caterpillar, dangling before me. Maybe it's due to the wine, or Rosanna's words stirring up so much imagery, but the hymns of my district start to echo in my ears.

I lift my gaze and imagine the glorious banner of the noble *contrada*—its heraldic caterpillar surmounting a pink rose, its field of yellow and green bound by an elegant blue border—being hurled skyward by our virtuoso flag throwers in their impressive medieval costumes. And I wish—just for a moment—that the silence of the Chianti morning might be broken by the rhythm of the drums our younger members beat with so much skill and passion . . .

Why the Caterpillar?

Many people ask me how a Wimbledon-born, Chianti-reared man, whose parents aren't originally from the area, came to be so involved in the medieval tradition of the Palio. After all, to be a member of a *contrada* you should be born in Siena; it is the specific place of birth within the city walls that for many years determined an infant's *contrada* affiliation. In the past babies were often delivered at home so that they would automatically become members of the district where their families lived. But not everyone was so conscientious, which is why there are families in which not every member was of same *contrada*. The father could, for example, be a member of the *Istrice* (Porcupine), the mother of the *Drago* (Dragon), and they could end up purchasing a house in the *Oca* (Goose) district; consequently their children would belong to that *contrada* if born at home.

In more recent times most Siena babies have been born in in the children's hospital located in the *Selva* (Forest) district, which would, if the old rules were observed, make all these newborns member of that *contrada* . . . which would of course be ridiculous. The tradition was therefore amended so that children are normally considered members of the district their parents live in. Still, some fathers have actually taken dirt from their own streets and deposited it under the maternity bed, so that they could announce that their child had been born on their *contrada*'s soil.

Once you belong to a *contrada*, you are a member for life. It's rare to switch to another, but cases have occurred, and the motives must be valid.

In modern times many Sienese have moved to the new buildings and apartment complexes outside the ancient city walls; because the *contrada* territories remain located within, however, children are often made members of the *contrada* that is closest to the family's house, making the districts located immediately inside the perimeter larger and consequently creating problems for the more centrally located ones whose populations are shrinking dramatically. This is one of the realities modern Siena has to face, as an increasingly large percentage of Sienese from all seventeen districts relocate to housing on the outskirts of town.

Upon arriving in Italy in the late 1970s, I was immediately intrigued by the Palio. My village companions weren't involved much, but the echoes of the event always reached us, and everybody would at least follow the race on TV. When at fourteen I started going to high school in Siena, most of my classmates were Sienese and obviously *contradaioli*. I was surprised to see that they all wore some sign of their affiliation, be it a ring, a necklace, or a bracelet. When invited to their homes, I realized that this branding wasn't limited to a few pieces of jewelry: Many household objects bore the same symbols.

One day I was invited by a school friend named Riccardo to study at his house. I can well remember his bedroom; it was completely covered with *Pantera* (Panther) posters and filled with stickers. And the color scheme throughout was that *contrada*'s distinctive red and blue. His mother, Rita, was a *Leocorno* (Unicorn), and to my surprise even the plates on which she served us lunch were orange and blue and decorated with little unicorns around the rims.

When Riccardo's father parked in front of the house later that afternoon, we walked to the porch to greet him, and I noticed that his Fiat was covered with the bumper stickers and badges of the *Bruco* (Caterpillar). When he shook my hand, I saw he wore an enormous ring with his *contrada*'s mascot engraved in the center.

In the evening, after finishing his homework, my friend would regularly visit his district headquarters and spend his free time with his *Pantera* companions, learning the art of tossing the flag in the air and playing the drums. He also played in the local *Pantera* soccer team, and would even go on vacation with his *Pantera* companions. His dream was to be chosen to participate in the parade that precedes the Palio as an *alfiere* (flag waver).

We spent the evening with his parents talking about past races and the fistfights they had all participated in against the members of their enemy *contrade*. "But if the *Pantera* is the rival of the *Aquila*," I asked, "how is it possible that you sit next to one at school in class?" Riccardo explained that he and Simone were actually very good friends; just because Simone was a member of a rival *contrada* didn't mean he had to cultivate hostility toward the boy *personally*. True, he was officially an enemy, and during the days preceding the previous year's Palio the *Panteras* and the *Aquile did* have a huge brawl in the square, during which he and Simone had exchanged a few blows. But this was all done without hard feelings, and days later they met for a drink on the square as though nothing had happened, each boasting a shiner around one eye.

"That's the Palio," he explained with an open-armed shrug.

Riccardo's father then told me of a famous incident in which the *Nicchio* (Shell) and the *Montone* (Ram), two of the greatest rivals in town, were both taking their horses into the square for a trial run, and being neighbors they accidentally arrived at the same intersection at the same time. With neither about to give way to the other, verbal taunting escalated into fisticuffs, and the inevitable melee broke out. After several minutes one of the Ram members cried, "Stop!" and the brawl came to an unexpected halt. All eyes turned to the distraught Ram member, who explained, "I lost my ring—the one with the symbol of my *contrada* engraved on it!" Everybody from both *contrade* crouched down and started scouring the street for the precious object. Finally a member of the *Nicchio* discovered it, handed it to the *Montone* member, waited for his rival to replace the ring on his finger—then punched him in the face. And the brawl instantly took up where it had left off, with no loss of passion.

Weeks later, the brawlers would also have likely sat down with a bottle of *vino* and laughed about the incident. There would be no retaliation; in this way, the Palio is unique. "That is the magic of Siena," Riccardo's father concluded proudly, "and it explains why sociologists come from all over the world to study the Palio."

When I started my career as a tour guide many years later, I was convinced that it was impossible to comprehend Siena's medieval spirit without some understanding of this annual event; and so I decided that a tour of Siena wouldn't be complete without paying a visit to a *contrada*'s private base of operations. The headquarters of all seventeen districts are quite beautiful, each displaying the medieval costumes worn in the parades and, even more spectacularly, all the Palio banners won in the past centuries, many of them works of art.

The problem is that these headquarters are open to the public only on the night of a victory, when the small halls are completely jammed with sweaty (and often drunk) visitors. At any other time of year, obtaining entry can be daunting. An additional problem for me was that my groups normally consisted of two or three people, so I couldn't offer large sums of money to bribe our way in. I did try, though; I made appointments to visit each *contrada's economo* (museum curator), but as I had expected, I met with little success. One after another was reluctant to open his doors to me. I had practically given up hope when I reached the last *contrada* on my list, the *Tartuca* (Tu rtle), and found myself shaking hands with a charming old man called Nanni.

With nothing to lose, this time I changed tactics. Knowing that the Sienese are very superstitious, I simply said, "Nanni, your *contrada* hasn't won the Palio for eighteen years. If you open the doors of the museum to my guests, I promise I will bring you luck."

To my surprise, Nanni took my words very seriously. He gave me his phone number and said, "Dario, whenever you need me, just call, and I'll come and open the doors for you." As I drove home that evening, I was delighted at the deal I'd struck—but then it dawned on me what a great responsibility I'd taken on. I'd promised Nanni something I couldn't possibly guarantee.

I did take advantage of Nanni's hospitality, though, and in 1991 often took guests to visit the Turtle headquarters. As the July Palio approached, I became anxious. Fortunately, on June 29, the *Tartuca* drew a great horse and engaged Cianchino, a top jockey, to ride. Even so, I remained apprehensive; anything could happen—and in Siena usually does.

The day of the Palio I was all wired up, but due to heavy rainfall the race was postponed to the following day. Another day in an agony of waiting. Yet ultimately I was rewarded: On July 3,

1991, the *Tartuca* triumphed in its first victory since 1972.

With my girlfriend of that time, Simona, I watched the race on at her house in the *Lupa* (She-wolf) district, and as soon as it ended I burst out into the streets and dashed across town to the Turtle *contrada*, where I found Nanni weeping. As soon as he saw me he pulled me into a warm embrace and sobbed on my shoulder for a seemingly endless ten minutes. All he could say was "Thank you, Dario, thank you!" My shirt was drenched in sweat and tears. I was invited as an honorary guest to all the victory celebrations and became very popular among the *Tartuca contrada* members—Nanni had spread the word about my promise. In the following years the headquarter doors were flung open for me whenever I wished to visit.

In 1992 the *Tartuca* didn't race; in 1993 it ran in both July and August without luck; then in 1994, it was selected to race the August Palio. Their horse wasn't a favorite, but against the odds the Turtle won again, dominating the three laps with Delfort Song and *Bufera* (Hurricane), the jockey. This time Nanni and many others in the *contrada* offered me membership. I was honored indeed, but somehow wasn't persuaded it was right for me; for the moment, I preferred to remain neutral.

The Turtle museum then closed for renovation: Because they had no empty wall for their new Palio banner, they decided to enlarge the headquarters. Suddenly I was without a headquarters to show my clients. Nanni very kindly came to my aid, calling a friend of the *Onda* (Wave) *contrada* and telling him how my presence had brought two victories for the *Tartuca*. The *Onda* opened their doors to me.

By this time I was getting tired of hosting tours of Siena, so that year I took advantage of the *Onda*'s hospitality only twice. Again, the incredible occurred: After a ten-year dry spell, *Onda* won the July Palio with Oriolo de Zamaglia and (again) the jockey Cianchino. I just couldn't believe my luck!

As the news spread, I started receiving invitations from many people to go and visit their *contrade*. In 1996 a *Chiocciola* (Snail) member offered me dinner in his district—but because they are the rivals of the *Tartuca*, out of respect for Nanni I politely declined. Still, I accepted the invitation of the unluckiest *contrada* of Siena, the Noble *Contrada* of the *Bruco* (Caterpillar), aka *la nonna* (the grandmother) district: They hadn't won a Palio since 1955—and prior to that 1922.

For some reason this district had always appealed to me, and every time I walked its streets I felt a kind of magical attraction. Most of its members had yet to experience a victory; many were convinced they might never see one in their lifetime. In 1996 some Caterpillar friends took me to the lottery selection of the horses, and were tremendously excited when they drew what appeared to be one of the best. The *contrada* then hired Cianchino, whose victories for the Turtle and the Wave had been so crucial for me.

The *contrada* also offered me dinner the night before the race, at the traditional banquet (a sit-down dinner for 1,700 people!). There we drank red wine and discussed previous Palios into the wee hours of the night. My friends explained that the *Bruco* had often been lucky with the drawing of the horse, but then something during the race had always gone wrong. It was as if they were under some kind of terrible curse.

In previous centuries the Caterpillar had won a fair number of Palios; even the twentieth century had started generously, with two close victories in 1907 and 1912, then an acceptable ten-year pause before winning again in 1922. But then . . . something happened, as thirty-three interminable years passed before a Palio again entered *Bruco* headquarters. And it was now forty-one years since *that* victory . . . forty-one years of tears and frustrations and dashed hopes.

My heart went out to these people, and I promised myself that whatever happened the following day, if they would accept me, I would become one of them. I then pulled out a piece of paper and wrote down *7/12/22/55*—the sequence of *Bruco* victory years that century—and stared at it for hours, as though the numbers had something they might reveal to me.

At 5:00 A.M. I drove home to my village to get some sleep. The following day I would return to Sienna where I had rented a room with a window overlooking the square for some guests of mine, and I wanted to be in reasonably good shape by the time we met there to watch the race. I woke up at 11:00 A.M., a little groggy, but as I was shaving my mind cleared and returned to the Caterpillar victory years. Suddenly struck by an idea, I swiped my finger through the shaving cream on my face and started to write the numbers on the mirror. When I had completed the column, I added them up: 7 + 12 + 22 + 55 . . . equals 96!

I started to tremble, so much so that it was difficult to finish shaving without cutting myself. This couldn't be a coincidence, could it? . . . I'd been so sure the numbers were trying to tell me something, and now they had.

Just before leaving my apartment, I donned the green-and-yellow Caterpillar scarf. All the way to Siena, I reflected on the numbers, the omen, the great importance to me of whatever happened that day. When I reached the *campo*, I was knotted up with tension. I could barely speak to my guests; my throat was dry and my voice hoarse.

Usually I enjoy the parade of youths in medieval and Renaissance costumes that precedes every Palio, but today the procession seemed endless. When, after the usual nerve-racking jockeying for position at the starting line, the race finally began, the *Bruco* suffered a terrible start and was in last place. But on the second lap Cianchino, the jockey, began really pushing the horse, and after a few breathtaking moves he started overtaking the other riders. By the third lap he was, amazingly, in the lead—and then, just like that, we had won! The *Bruco* had broken its decades-long losing streak!

Leaving my guests at the window, I ran out of the building and into the square where I joined with the other hundreds of *Brucos* in screaming, crying, and howling with joy. We claimed the Palio banner and carried it to the Duomo for the post-race thanksgiving, then paraded it through the streets all night long, drinking and singing. The celebrations went on for days, then weeks, and finally months; in all, we had forty-one victory dinners, one for each year of defeat. The district streets remained lit like a carnival, gallons of wine vanished down members' throats, and every evening until November we marched through the city with drums beating and flags waving.

On August 16, 1996, I became a real Sienese, a proud member of the *Bruco*, an active *contradaiolo*, and a member of the society that organizes the banquets, feasts, and all kinds of social events. Today I volunteer to help in the *Bruco* kitchen when we have dinners, participate in *Bruco* assemblies, help organize *Bruco* feasts, play on the *Bruco* soccer team, participate in the *Bruco* jogging club—whatever opportunity is offered. I also, of course, take part in the passionate discussions of horses and past Palios. I can never thank the *contrada* enough for accepting me into their big family.

We won again in August 2003, July 2005 and August 2008... but that's another story.

10:08 A.M.

I'm now heading toward one of my favorite spots. I've nearly reached the top of the hill. From there the views are almost 360 degrees and . . . well, in my opinion the word *spectacular* is inadequate.

Arriving at my destination, I choose to sit on the ancient remains of an old stone wall built far in the past to terrace the fields. I'm looking southward toward Siena, which, thanks to this pristine morning, is easily distinguished by its characteristic burnt-red bricks. The vista is dominated by the towers of the Duomo and the town hall, symbols of the city's glorious medieval past. The architects even managed to make the tower tops level with each other, despite the structures that support them being built on different gradients. This was done to demonstrate that the institutions they represented were equally important.

The contrasts in this area are stunning. Chianti is mostly lovely rolling woodland that begins just south of Florence and extends all the way to Siena. Then just south of the city, acting almost as a watershed, commences the Crete Senesi—endless hills of gray clay sown with wheat and sunflowers. This landscape abruptly terminates at the foot of Monte Amiata, an ancient volcano; again the terrain is predominantly wooded, with thick chestnut forests. The highest point of the entire province, this is a winter ski resort.

Just below me I spot a figure climbing the steep ravine. A moment later, and I recognize her. It's Piera . . .

Piera

As is her habit, Piera has been out all morning collecting dry branches to store as fuel for the following winter's fires. She carries them in a wicker basket on her back, held by a thick rope stretched over her shoulder and clasped firmly in both of her ancient, trembling weathered hands. She also collects wild herbs, which she digs from the ground with a pocket spade attached to her leather belt.

She sees me and slowly makes her way over. She lowers the wicker basket to the ground, unties the knot beneath her chin that releases her black silk scarf, and kisses me on my cheek with her cold, dry lips. As she sits next to me, I pluck a wild lily, disturbing a bee that's been buzzing around its stamen, and hand it to her; she smiles, revealing a mouth completely devoid of teeth. I look at her forehead, a relief map of wrinkles, and contemplate this unlikely and long-missed friend of mine.

Piera lives in the village with her son, a successful lawyer, and his family. For some time they were critical of her daily country escapades, reminding her that there was no need for her to waste her energy picking twigs: They had central heating, and Checco could always deliver firewood in his truck. But eventually they gave up. Piera is a stubborn old lady, and she enjoys spending her days in the rocky fields . . . and time enjoyed is never really time wasted. As if to demonstrate this, she hands me a bunch of wild lettuce as a gift, reminding me to wash it thoroughly under cold water when I get home and even suggesting I eat it with a drop of oil and balsamic vinegar.

"Where have you been, Dariolino?" she says, protecting her eyes from the sun with her bony hands. "I haven't seen you for a while."

"I was in America, Piera."

"L'Ammerica Caspiterina!" she exclaims, using a colorful but lost local expression. "Me, I've never been beyond Poggibonsi." She laughs while jabbing her little finger westward, in the direction of the grubby industrial town tucked at the bottom of the valley and lapped by the Elsa River.

She then points out a recently restored old farmhouse partly hidden by a cypress forest; it's now rented as a vacation home for tourists. "I was born right there," she says proudly. "Isn't it a beautiful spot? To think that I lived in that house for more than half a century until the great industrialization occurred, and suddenly our world vanished! We all just up and left, moving to the towns, where we were firmly convinced we would live a better life. Even today I wonder if it was the right choice. Sure, we were poor, but only in terms of this"—she rubs her thumb and index finger together in the gesture indicating money. "Everything else about our lives was so intense and so full, so though we had nothing, in a certain way we had everything. You know, Dariolino, *si stava meglio quando si stava peggio*"—we were better off when we were worst off.

"We owned nothing ourselves," she continues. "The fields our men plowed belonged to the landowner, as did the farmhouse and the animals, and in a certain way so did we! Life for a child was tough—we had chores and duties that filled almost every moment—but we also had lots of fun and found many ways to entertain ourselves. I feel so sorry when I see my grandchildren sit for hours in front of the *homputet*"—she pronounces the word for computer in the local dialect—"their glassy eyes staring endlessly at that screen, wasting their time messing around with those plastic sticks and buttons and producing all those funny noises. The children in my family were responsible for raising the silkworms and looking after the pigeons. Their cooing was a constant soundtrack of my childhood, as they nested in the attic right above our bedrooms, which were on the top floor."

She raises her head and gazes into the blue, watching intently as the swallows veer and dive into the valleys. "I always loved swallows," she continues warmly. "There used to be thousands, not like today when you only ever see a small flock, and that if you're lucky. We longed so much to see them, because it meant that summer was close at hand. When they disappeared each winter, Uncle told me that they were flying to Africa. I had no idea were that was; now I know, and it's hard to think of those little creatures traveling even farther than you, Dariolino!" She turns her gaze back to me and smiles.

"Our farmhouse was very large because it had to fit many families; we shared it with many relatives. I can't remember the number exactly, but Mother had all her six brothers and sisters living with us, and they were all married and they all had children. Also there were both my grandparents, so just imagine how many of us lived down there!" She tries to tally them using her fingers, then gives up.

"Obviously nobody had their own bedroom," she goes on. "We all had to share them with other people of our same age and sex, and privacy was not even a word to us. We had many fireplaces in our house, but we never lit them all at the same time, as we didn't want to waste the firewood. *Waste* was another word that just wasn't part of our vocabulary. The most common rule was *Un si butta via niente*"—we don't throw anything away.

Remembering the hardships, she continues, "Parsimony meant survival, waste meant starvation. Not even the ashes left in the fireplace were discarded—we used them to make the *ranno,* our detergent. The women would collect the ashes and place them on a thick linen cloth. Then they would place the dirty laundry above a large terra-cotta container and pour on boiling water, which would filter through the cloth and fill the large pot. When the clothes were well soaked, the women would spill out the water and scrub them energetically. They would do this several times. The results were incredible, the clothes were immaculate, better than any of those industrial soaps my daughter-in-law buys at the supermarket.

"Also, the hot embers from the fireplace were placed in tin containers that our grandmothers would place underneath the sheets; when we went to bed, we could snuggle in and enjoy the warmth. The container was called *il prete* [the priest], don't ask me why, Dariolino. I remember I shared the bed with my younger cousin and sister, and often we would talk until very late at night. We would take turns in making up bedtime stories before drifting off to a sound sleep." I decide not to interrupt Piera, as she seems willing to talk and I am more than willing to listen. Also, the soft singsong of her narration is such a pleasure to hear.

"In the morning we were awakened by the aroma of baking bread, whose crusty surface Auntie would spread with blackberry jam using a crude kitchen knife. One of the children's chores was to collect the berries from the prickly bushes. I remember one hot summer day when I was picking those juicy, ripe fruits. I tripped and fell into the bush. I ran home in tears, my skirt torn and my face and arms covered with tiny little cuts. I still recall how they hurt, those little wounds on my soft young skin, and how Gran soothed them by rubbing them with a salve she had made out of beeswax, olive oil, and some other mysterious ingredients. She had remedies for everything, and made ointments from all kinds of weeds and wildflowers. For more serious diseases she used jackrabbit blood, chicken droppings, and live lice, and many people would come to see her because her skill was known all through the hills. According to my father, the best way to disinfect a wound was to pee on it. Once when he was harvesting the wheat, he cut himself with the sickle, and he did so without hesitation in front of us all!"

Piera, her toothless smile still in place, plunges deeper into her memory with increasing passion. "We used to walk for miles—we had no other means of transportation. Every week we would go and sell our goods in the market in Siena. I would accompany my uncles, who pushed their wooden carts, loaded to the brim, up and down the steep hills. They were so strong, and had muscles and wills of iron. Often we would stop and recite a prayer in front of the shrines we found along the paths, and I would place wildflowers, picked just for this purpose, before of the image of the Madonna. The walk took many hours, but we were never in a rush, and on the way we always met other travelers and often talked all the way to our common destination and back. Even time itself was different, it seems; the days were so much longer, they seemed to last forever. Is it possible that the hours have gotten shorter nowadays?" I start to reply that this is impossible, but with a wink Piera shows me that she is only joking.

"There was always some woman pregnant in the house, and obviously the newly born were always delivered in their beds. Alas, infant mortality was rather high, and I lost count of how many children's funerals I assisted in those days. For some reason it seemed that our women always delivered their babies at night. I remember the shrieks of Mother and her sisters filling up the silent nights, and we children listening, huddled together beneath the blankets; when the shrieks suddenly ceased we anxiously waited for a grown-up come into our room, bearing a candle, to tell us with a smiling face whether we had a new boy or girl in the house. This was always a moment of joy, although we knew we had to share our bread with another newcomer. Often an enormous-breasted wet nurse from some poorer family came and stayed with us, and sometimes I felt very sorry for them. They grew very fond of the babies, but once the children were weaned, the nurses had to return to their homes.

"Despite our isolation our *podere* [farm] was always full of visitors. Many *vagabondi* [tramps] would come by and do some odd jobs in exchange for a bowl of soup. They would sleep in the barn or the stables with the cows, and some of them were very colorful indeed. I remember that many traveled with an accordion tied to their backs, and often were the most delightful musicians, entertaining us during those long summer nights when we would dance *liscio* on the worn-out terra-cotta tiles in the chicken yard. All that these men got in exchange for their labors was a bed and a hot meal, then they would return to their hills with a flask of wine and a bottle of oil. They had no obligations to us, no timetables—we were all free spirits.

"I remember one *vagabondo* in particular who would tell me many tales about his travels. He fibbed that he had walked all the way to China and had entertained many emperors and their courts with his trusty instrument, and for this reason we called him Marco Polo. He was definitely one of our favorites. He would come every year, but one summer he failed to show up. We never saw him again, nor ever found out what happened. In my childhood fancy, I imagined him entertaining all kinds of kings and queens in some faraway, exotic country."

Piera falls silent for a moment. I imagine she is still thinking about Marco Polo, whom I guess she was possibly more than just simply fond of by the loving expression on her face, though her gaze still points firmly in the direction of the old farmhouse that had been the theater of her childhood.

Finally she speaks again. "Apart from the *vagabondi,* a couple of *treccoloni* [peddlers] would periodically pay us a visit and try to sell or exchange their goods, which usually consisted of cloth, needles, strings, and elastics. Bino was the funniest. He would peddle from farm to farm on his trusty, rusty, bulky bike that had no brakes, and would come to a halt by dragging his enormous feet on the rough surface of the yard, raising a cloud of dust. He was tall and wiry and his pants were made of a very thick woolen material, stitched with patches; they were so heavy, the crotch would fall well below his knees—he looked like a clown. He wore a *picciotto*-style cap that he pulled down over his forehead, partly covering his eyes, but what was most extraordinary was that he had the ability to speak exclusively in rhyme—even when replying to our own comments. He was mocked by our men, but I think that's because they were a bit envious of him. He was one of the very few men—along with the local priest—who met lots of women alone, since he always arrived at the farms when the other men were off working the fields."

Piera now turns away from her old house, toward me; she seems a bit surprised to find me enjoying her memories so much, but when she sees that I am, she smiles and goes on. "School was not mandatory and it was very far to reach, but fortunately my parents wanted me to read and write. And so together with my brothers, sisters, cousins, and friends from nearby farms I would trek several miles to school each day. In the winter it was tough having to cross the frozen fields, but in the spring it was great fun to walk back home with all my friends. Sometimes we would stop by the creek and have a swim. And we never returned home empty handed; we always collected many wonderful things en route. Our aunt Talia made wicker baskets from dried twigs for us. Depending on the season we filled these brimful with chestnuts, arbutus, porcini mushrooms, wild strawberries, blackberries, bilberries, juniper berries, raspberries, wild garlic, wild fennel, chamomile, and—my mother's favorite—wild asparagus, which she liked fried in omelets. The boys also mastered the art of capturing frogs in the creek, and the belief was that they were tastier during the months that did not contain an *r*—don't ask me why, Dariolino, I have no answer. When they brought them home, the women skinned them and then kept them in water with nettles to purify them of the mud. Then they were fried in olive oil—a delicacy. So were the big juicy snails, which we cooked in spicy tomato sauce!

"Now, our elders never attended school, so you'd think they must be rather ignorant. On the contrary. During the long winter evenings when it got dark early, we would sit around the large fireplace in the kitchen and they would entertain us by reciting poems that they had learned by heart; some lasted for hours. It was beautiful to look at the expressions on their animated faces, lit up by the reflections of the glowing embers. Many smoked pipes that released a sweet aroma; then their contents were emptied into the fire. Nothing wasted, eh? . . . My great-uncle was able to recite by heart entire passages from the *Divina Commedia* and the *Odyssey,* which he did while twitching the tips of his mustache with his gigantic callused fingers.

"My mother was very patient and sweet and seldom scolded us. She had hair black as pitch, and light blue eyes that sparkled even more than usual when she sang a cappella the simple songs she improvised while working in the kitchen. During weddings she was able to reduce the entire church congregation to tears with her intense interpretation of Schubert's 'Ave Maria.' *Babbo* [Dad], on the other hand, was never was very talkative with his daughters; I remember him as bald and stubborn, even when he was younger. Like most men of that generation, he had fought in the Great War and had lost two brothers and many friends in those terrible battles." Abruptly Piera stops and makes the sign of the cross in memory of her lost parents. This is the first time she's stopped smiling. A moment later she caresses my hair and continues.

"Of all the people living in the house, my favorite was my younger cousin Giulio. He was a rascal, constantly getting into trouble, and he played many jokes and pranks on all of us. His specialty was to hide snakes under our aunt's bedsheets, and he'd often startle us by pulling out of his pocket some tiny mouse or lizard that he had raised himself. In the Second World War he was called for duty and sent to fight in Russia, and during Italy's disastrous retreat in 1943 we stopped receiving letters from him. Eventually, like many other thousands, he was considered *disperso* and we slowly gave up hope. Then one lazy summer evening, a few years after the war had ended, while we were having our meal [around a wooden table beneath the shade of an acacia tree, we spotted a figure slowly coming up from the rows of Sangiovese in the vineyard, just ambling toward us with his hands in his pockets. As the mysterious character approached, we could hear him softly whistling a tune. We all observed him in silence, and when he was a few yards away, he raised his hat, dried the beads of sweat from his forehead with his forearm, and in a casual tone this thin, long-bearded stranger said, 'Can you offer me a glass of red, please?'

"Mother started screaming, and seconds later we all realized it was Giulio! He had been taken prisoner, and after his release had patiently walked all the way home from Russia! I think that was the most touching moment of my life, Dariolino, as we all embraced him, and broke down and wept. Only Giulio remained completely unfazed, as if he had simply been away a few hours for a short stroll around the woods." Piera's eyes suddenly redden; she pulls a handkerchief from her sleeve and blows her nose, then dries her eyes with her knuckles, tucks the hankie back into her sleeve, and changes the subject.

"We had stables on the bottom floor of the farmhouse, filled with animals. Imagine us living above it—the air that we breathed constantly filled with the smell of manure. For us it was just normal, and only years later did I realize that we carried those foul smells with us wherever we went! I wonder what names the elegant *signori* in Siena gave us when they purchased our goods at the markets?

"I remember with mixed emotions the times we had to slaughter a pig. The animal is very sensitive, you know, and apparently when sentenced to death knows his fate in advance. I had the firm conviction that the night before his execution I could hear the pig weep softly from my open window. The following day was even worse; it was always heartbreaking to watch him dragged out of the pen, emitting shrieks of desperation. I had to cover my ears and hide. Uncle Fabio, who was our *norcino,* would then slit the poor beast's throat, and with the help of the other men turn the carcass upside down and open it up with the precision of a surgeon. Not one single part of the animal went wasted; we ate every inch of the body—including the ears," Piera explains. "Gran made the most mouthwatering *migliacci*—a mixture of pig's blood, stale bread, sugar, orange peels, walnuts, and flour that we downed with a drop of the precious, sweet *vin santo* drawn directly from the *caratello* chestnut barrel in front of the fireplace.

"I was rather scared of the pigs. There was a legend around our hills of a man who, on his way home after getting drunk at the local *osteria,* accidentally fell into the stockyard and was gobbled up. Only days later, while cleaning up the pen, did someone find his wedding ring and realize what had happened to poor Edoardo. Can you imagine, Dariolino, the ring was all that remained of him! I never really believed this story," she concludes. "I think the grown-ups made it up to frighten me away from the pigpen."

Piera now seems lost in memory; it flows over her in waves. I'm thrilled to be on the receiving end. As we say in Tuscany, *stava sfondando una porta aperta*—she's broken through an open door.

"One of my fondest periods of the year was the wheat harvest in August. It was hard work, and yet another occasion to be all together and collect the fruits of our sweat. Imagine entire armies of men and women working in those fields under the hot sun! Even so, there were no timetables to follow. We worked early in the morning, took a long break when the sun was at its peak, then continued in the evening until sunset. You know, Dariolino, even the heat and the cold were more intense than nowadays. We would kill time telling jokes and gossiping about our neighbors. Only the olive harvest in December I dreaded, because sometimes it was cold, tedious work and I was afraid of falling from the trees."

Now Piera picks up a handful of soil and observes it, then lets it crumble from her hand. "The Chianti soil is bitter, arid, and rocky. It gives very little, but what it does produce is of the highest quality, and with care we managed to be self-sufficient. The only product that the soil of these hills ever offers in abundance is wine.

"Definitely the late-September *vendemmia* [grape harvest] was the most enjoyable time of the year. You know the importance wine had in our life: It was fundamental. Wine was by no means just a drink. It was as important as bread for us, a vital source of nourishment. It gave us our vitamin C; it was our seniors' anti-aging elixir; it was our water disinfectant, our antidepressant, our magic potion for strength when we did the heavy work, our everything. At breakfast Mother would dip stale bread in red wine and add a pinch of sugar. It was divine! And if we were ill, what better remedy than hot wine and spices? And of course at lunch and dinner we downed liters of it! It had a different taste than today: It was simply fermented grape juice that we drank young without aging. Despite how much of it we consumed, we never got a headache or woke up the following morning with a hangover.

"The other day while returning home, I passed by Paolo's *enoteca* and spotted an elegant gentleman holding an enormous crystal goblet that contained a small amount of wine. I watched him awhile. He kept twirling it around and sticking his nose in it. I had no idea what he was doing, though he kept at it for minutes. Then he took a small sip, emitted all kinds of guttural sounds, and to my horror spat it all out into a small container. I watched him repeat the entire operation with another wine poured from another bottle, and when I saw him spit it again I left in disgust. My father, I thought, would have been appalled—fancy spitting out that nectar!" Her eyes are dancing, but she is very serious. "He used to keep a flask of wine at the end of the row of vineyards when working the fields, and when he finished pruning a row he rewarded himself with a swig directly from the *fiasco* before going on to tackle the next. He hated water; he said it was good only for the perverted and that the flood proved it. I never knew what he really meant by that phrase, but the way he declared it left no doubt that he was very sure of its significance!"

Suddenly Piera stops short and exclaims, "*Caspiterina!*" [Good Heavens!]. She's a little embarrassed that she's let herself run on so, and has remembered she must now go and prepare lunch for her grandchildren. "Dariolino," she says as she dons her scarf again, "I've noticed you often come here at night in the summer."

I nod. "I love watching the fireflies."

"Ah, the fireflies," Piera cries, delightedly clapping her thin hands. "They are marvelous, such mysterious creatures. When I was young, we would look out my window, and the valleys were so full of them it seemed as if the stars had fallen to the ground, or the sky had tipped like a bucket and poured them all out. Oh, there were so many in those days! That period for me was the era of the fireflies, Dariolino." She picks up her basket, kisses me on the cheek, and heads down toward the village. I follow her with my eyes, contemplating her long and wonderful life, impoverished in many ways, but rich in so many others. I find myself envying her life in the era of fireflies.

11:13 A.M.

I decide to sit another few minutes on the stone wall. A few bright green lizards are busy chasing one another nearby. I've always wondered whether this is a game or some territorial dispute—but it's impossible to tell from observation. Like all reptiles they have no expressions.

The olive trees have recently been pruned, and their branches scatter around their trunks like shorn hair, ready to be gathered and burned. The sparrows are singing, collecting food for their little ones, and I also spot a magnificent hoopoe fluttering high above. I find this bird by far the most elegant we have on these hills, so stylish it seems the creation of one of our great Italian fashion designers. It's a shy bird; farmers have told me it's impossible to tame, and also gives off a very unpleasant odor.

I hear the crunch of tires and turn to see the mailman's van climbing the hill. He stops and greets me. "Dario, welcome back! Does this mean I can deliver you the mail again? I have a few cartons of letters from the United States, what's been going on? You're receiving more mail than the entire village put together." He winks. Judging by his rosy cheeks and nose, he's been drinking again—and the way he now zigzags over the hazardous road is all but confirmation.

He's scarcely out of sight when it's my good friend Giovanni's turn to drive up and greet me. "*Ciao*, Dario—ready for a pizza at Bianca's this week? We're all dying to hear about your trip! I'll book for Friday, bring your photos." I agree, telling him to round up the gang for a reunion. As he drives off to the winery where he's employed, it occurs to me that I have no photos to show my friends: I didn't take any.

Giovanni was a successful lawyer in Milan, but left that stressful vocation and the fast pace of city life to work as a laborer in the vineyards of Chianti. He's never regretted his courageous choice. A few years ago he purchased from me my glorious little four-wheel-drive van, the one in which I'd escorted all my first clients around Tuscany. I'm glad he still possesses it—glad and a little melancholy . . .

A Van for All Seasons

Over its sixteen years, my beloved van caused as many problems as it solved. The Subaru four-wheel drive was indeed a great little vehicle—but very little indeed. It was designed to seat five, plus the driver, but the Japanese designers seem to have had Japanese passengers in mind—and not of the sumo variety.

Some years ago I received an e-mail from a family in the United States who were hoping to engage my services for a countryside tour, and also if possible my help in organizing a brief cooking class. They had booked a Florence hotel in a pedestrian-only area close to the Uffizi art gallery. So to avoid getting a ticket, I asked if they would kindly cross the River Arno and meet me on the other side of the Ponte Vecchio, where I would be waiting for them at the taxi stop.

They consented, and so on a rather dull April morning I drove to Florence and waited for them at the appointed spot. As is my custom, I arrived early and sat on the wall overlooking the riverbanks, killing time by observing a group of nutrias swimming in the mud-colored water. I find these large rodents to be rather cute; they look much like beavers except in the tail, which unfortunately is more ratlike than the wide, flat model their cousins possess. They are not native to Italy but were imported from North America for their fur; apparently many escaped the farms and, with no natural predators, multiplied rapidly all along the Tuscan riverbanks. While I idly watched one dig a hole on the sandy bed, I noticed in the distance a group of four people coming up the street in my direction. Presuming them to be the family I was to meet, I turned my attention from the nutria to study them before they arrived. I couldn't help noticing that they were all extremely large, and because of their size they were moving slowly. Also, despite the hotel being just minutes away, they kept stopping for breathers.

I could now see by the inquisitive expressions on their faces that they were expecting someone to appear to greet them. They must indeed be my clients. I jumped off the wall and walked up with my hand extended. "Hello, I'm Dario, your guide."

Their faces brightened. I suddenly found myself in charge of the physically largest family I had ever seen. Even the effort of shaking my hand had them panting as if they'd just run the Boston Marathon.

When the mother shook my hand, her fingers felt like five little *cacciatorino* salamis. Next to her was her daughter, nearly as large and, like her mum, wearing a homemade-looking flowery pastel dress that covered her head-to-toe.

The father was larger still. He boasted an impressive ZZ Top–style beard and a pair of black sunglasses. Next to him, his son seemed almost small, and in fact he was the least massive of the group. It took more years than he'd lived to acquire the kind of girth his parents had.

Mike, the father, told me they were all set to go, and indeed by their huffing and puffing I could see they were more than ready to take a seat. But as soon as I pointed out the van to them, I realized what a task it would be to fit them inside.

I said nothing, pretending that all was perfectly normal as I pulled open the side sliding door, then lifted the row of middle seats to allow access to the back. "Okay," I said, "one of you in the back, two in the middle, and one rides up front next to me."

Sheila, the mother, decided to attempt the climb into the backseat. She grasped the grip with both hands to haul herself in. The vehicle rocked dangerously to one side, yet she somehow managed to squeeze herself into place. The sense of victory was short lived, however, for when I tried to lower the row of central seats into place they wouldn't go; they were obstructed by her knees.

After a few moments' stalemate, Sheila pulled up her legs and reclined on the seat, trying to convince me that she had no problem remaining in that position for the entire drive.

With Sheila in place, it was time to fill the two middle seats. It took the daughter a few minutes to climb aboard, but—as I'd expected—once she managed to get inside and wedge herself into place, she occupied both seats. In the meantime, Mike the dad had tried crawling into the front, but once he succeeded in getting his belly through, his backside got stuck between the doors. I was frantic by this time, and made several remarks on the hopelessness of the endeavor. My clients insisted it was still doable, and tried out many other solutions—this person there and that person here—but the results were always the same: One, often one and a half, of the family was stranded outside. As these attempts to fit in the van were getting underway, a small crowd of people gathered, laughing and applauding as though they thought we were engaged in some kind of circus act. If I had passed around a hat, I might have collected a fair amount of change.

After half an hour more of trying to defy the laws of physics, we decided the most sensible thing to do was call a colleague with a bus. They seemed very embarrassed by the extreme measures, and as we waited for my friend, they agreed among themselves to seriously consider dieting. Within minutes they were arguing which of them would lose the most weight the quickest, all the while devouring a king-sized pack of barbecue-flavored potato chips, washed down with cans of soda.

On another occasion I picked up a famous American basketball player who had just signed up for one of the top Italian teams. This time the problem was less volume than height. I suggested opening the sunroof so he wouldn't have to spend the entire drive crouched in the fetal position, and he was game. Fortunately it was a beautiful day, but the scene of me driving through the villages with the head of a 6-foot, 9-inch giant of a man craning from my roof must have been hilarious for the locals.

Still, my worst experience came on a cold day in late December. This was to be my last tour of the season, after which Cristina and I were leaving for a well-earned vacation in the tropics.

Normal routine, I thought that morning when I left the house to pick up a family of three in Florence. The road was covered with a light layer of frost that dissolved as soon as my tires passed over it, and a beautiful red sun appeared from the back of Pratomagno Mountain. I've driven this road countless times and never tire of at least the first part of it: Beautiful landscapes open behind each twisty curve before I turn onto the freeway.

When I reached the anonymous chain hotel, I found my clients, the Smiths, just finishing their breakfast and eager to set out. They were a very friendly young couple with a beautiful twelve-year-old daughter who wore her hair in a long braid her mother had probably fixed for her that morning with loving care. After the usual handshakes, they all filed enthusiastically into the van; I turned the heat to high and headed back toward my beloved hills, leaving the noisy city behind us.

Eventually we left the main road and turned onto a bumpy path full of potholes. Soon I noticed through the rearview mirror that Barbara, the little girl, no longer had those nice rosy cheeks . . . she was in fact looking pale. Minutes later Sarah, the mother, interrupted my introductory speech on Chianti to explain that Barbara was suffering from carsickness and asked if it was possible for me to slow down a little. This I did, assuring everyone that if they needed to stop, all they had do was ask.

The road remained irregular with many tight curves, and as we approached Radda in Chianti, Martin, the father—who had up to that moment been the most talkative of the group, impressed by the beautiful landscapes and filled with questions on the terrain and its history—suddenly went silent; he closed his eyes, placed his right hand on his stomach, and rolled down the window. I was getting a little worried, but apart from slowing down further there wasn't much I could do.

When we were about to reach our first stop, Barbara, who was now positively green, suddenly threw up her breakfast on the back of my neck, and almost simultaneously Martin covered his mouth with his right palm and puked on the dashboard. Sarah cried, "Oh dear, oh dear, Dario *stop*!"

I could feel the vomit trickle down the back of my head into my shirt. Hoping not to make things worse, I kept my mouth shut and pulled over on the deserted road, acting as though nothing extraordinary had happened. (It wasn't easy.) I told them not to worry, and suggested we all go and wash up in the small creek at the bottom of the hill.

Martin and I climbed down the ravine, cleaned up, and filled up a few bottles of ice-cold water for Barbarato use to wash up; by this time she was huddling miserably on the side of the road with her mother, who was in turn mortified by the whole situation. As we dried ourselves with some towels (which fortunately I always kept in the van), Barbara, still as pale as a starched sheet, said that she wanted to go back to the hotel: She was feeling very bad. Martin, who had recovered, thought that maybe this was the most sensible decision. And so, driving at a snail's pace and trying very hard to tackle the curves as smoothly as possible, we started back. Despite all the care her mother was giving, poor Barbara looked as if she was going to die; but the situation reached its nadir when Sarah, until then the only able-bodied member of the family, suddenly grabbed hold of a paper bag and, before I could stop the car, vomited into it.

When we finally reached the hotel, I left in the lobby three pale gray ghosts, their clothes soiled, apologetic tears in their eyes. I felt terrible for them, but managed to get a smile out of

Barbara when, to cheer her, I said that they had provided me with a chapter for my book.

And so they have.

11:47 A.M.

I'm now facing southeast. From here it's clear that the vast majority of the territory consists of thick, lush forests, a characteristic of Chianti unknown to most first-time visitors, who mainly notice the vineyards. Fortunately, it's now illegal to cut trees for development.

This thought comforts me. Thanks to these strict conservation laws, and should I be lucky enough to reach Piera's age, I will be able to stand exactly in this same spot and enjoy the same unspoiled views. How many times have I admired such magnificence? . . . How small and insignificant these scenes make me feel, confronting me with nature's power and majesty.

My gaze is now captured by a rare open space in the distance where the hills lower and give way to the Crete Senesi. I am looking toward Monteaperti, a field that was the theater of a medieval battle in which the Guelph faction, led by the Florentine army, fought the Sienese-backed Ghibbeline troops. The carnage that resulted was immortalized by Dante Alighieri in his eternal masterpiece, *La Divina Commedia* (The Divine Comedy), as having "dyed the river Arbia red with blood."

Today this vista fills my soul with such peace; I find it hard to imagine it once hosted bitter conflict and slaughter; but indeed, in the Middle Ages, peace here was nothing more than a dream. Over the centuries these hills have been drenched with the blood of thousands of soldiers, and the region's villages and castles have suffered destruction and looting for centuries. Even relatively recently my homeland endured terror and destruction during World War II.

Of all these battles, though, the mother of them all will always remain Monteaperti . . .

Remembering Monteaperti

Siena is without a doubt a city that thrives on the memories of its glorious past. The bond its citizens still feel with its illustrious medieval heritage is remarkable and reaches its apex during the Palio.

A focal moment of Sienna's history is certainly the battle at Monteaperti on September 4, 1260, when Siena so humiliated the Florentine army that even today the victory is used to taunt and ridicule Florence whenever the two cities clash. Attend any sporting event that pits Sienna and Florence against each other, and you can be sure the Sienese in the crowd will unveil banners reading REMEMBER MONTEAPERTI and other more inventive gibes. (At the last soccer game I attended, a club called "Those of Monteaperti" unfurled a banner reading MONTEAPERTI 1260: BEWARE BECAUSE I WAS THERE!)

Walking the streets in Siena, you can't help but notice how many are named after the heroes of that battle—those who commanded the Sienese battalions or had some other decisive role to play. You may also catch some relevant bumper stickers sailing by—perhaps MONTEAPERTI 1260, PROUD TO BE A GHIBBELINE.

Because the story has been passed from generation to generation for so many centuries, the facts and figures of the day have inevitably been inflated, and since the original documentation was so poor, it's difficult to know the battle's actual toll. So leaving aside my obvious pride in my Sienese heritage, and the romance and the legends that I have absorbed through the years, I decided to investigate the historical evidence. What follows is, as best I can determine, what happened on that infamous September day.

As the republic of Siena rose to prominence in the twelfth century, it came into direct competition with its prosperous neighbor Florence. In those days it was crucial for a city-state to control as much territory as possible, in order to expand its commerce, and clashes between the two powers were therefore inevitable.

During the first series of battles, it was usually Siena that was vanquished.

But nothing if not persistent, Siena finally managed in 1230 to prevail in battle and capture Montepulciano, an important city and center of commerce, and a source of contention between Siena and Florence. Siena defended Montepulciano in 1234 from a force comprised of Florentines, the army of Montalcino, and some local feudalists. In retaliation, the Florentines destroyed forty villages in Siena's territory, burned many wheat fields and vines, and returned to Florence with a huge booty and a small army of prisoners. Again Siena was forced to retreat from Montepulciano.

In 1250 Florence was seeking new avenues to the sea, and its attention fell on the Sienese ports of Talamone and Porto Ercole. For Florence to gain control of these towns would be a tremendous blow to any future ambitions Siena might have, and so the Sienese government allied with Arezzo, Pistoia, and Pisa—the latter a sea republic that already opposed Florence because it was allied with her enemy port city, Genoa. War broke out in 1251, and for two years Siena endured a series of calamitous defeats; in the end the city was forced to beg the Florentines for peace on hands and knees.

And thus the stage was set for the moment, nine years later, when Siena sent troops to the Maremma area to settle some insurgencies in their territories, and in so doing recaptured Grosseto on February 5, 1260. In the following months Siena also conquered Montemassi and Mensano, thanks to the help of Manfredi, the king of Sicily, who sent over a battalion of his German cavalier soldiers.

As a result of these conquests, Montalcino remained the only (Florentine) Guelph town within (Sienese) Ghibbeline territory. Fearing an imminent attack, Montalcino attempted to take in a store of provisions against a siege. But the German cavaliers were used to block trade routes and prevent supplies from reaching them.

It was time for Florence once more to come to the rescue. City officials sent an impressive army of 30,000 troops to go and help their Guelph allies, then suddenly changed their minds and turned the soldiers instead toward the city of Siena.

Siena was forced to recall its troops from Maremma. They found the formidable Florentine army camped less than a mile from the Sienese northern gate. When the Florentines were attacked by German troops on May 18, the latter were massacred, and the Florentines returned home with the emblem of King Manfredi of Sicily.

Over the following months the Sienese responded by devastating the town of Colle in the northern territories, then returning southward toward Maremma to lay siege to Montemassi and Montalcino. But Florence itself had been busy, organizing what was designed to be a final confrontation with Siena. In preparation, they had started diplomatic relationships with Riccardo, king of Cornovaglia, Corradino of Svevia, and Alfonso of Castiglia. They commenced gathering an impressive amount of food supplies to help Montalcino; on August 20, 1260, they moved their troops south.

Apparently, however, they were divided on which route to take. The military experts advised avoiding Siena, but the majority preferred to pass under the city's walls and taunt their enemy with this demonstration of power. On August 22 they camped in San Casciano; the following day just north of Castellina in Chianti, where the hotel Ricavo is today; and after that in the vicinity of Fonterutoli. Thus on August 30 they passed right below the hilltop where I now stand observing the view.

Instinctively I turn toward the road and try to imagine the scene: 3,000 cavaliers and 30,000 ground troops marching through, waving their banners and holding high their lances, probably singing battle songs. It must have been an impressive sight.

They put up their tents in Pievasciata, and apparently the Florentines sent some ambassadors to Siena, telling them to stop molesting Montalcino, and while they were at it to hand over the Florentine traitors who had converted to the Ghibbeline cause and taken refuge inside the walls of Siena. If these terms were not met, the Florentine forces threatened to spare no one, neither woman nor child; the city, they said, would be utterly demolished.

Despite the many defeats they had suffered, the Sienese were not intimidated, and simply replied that they would answer Florence on the field. The clash was thus inevitable . . . and it didn't augur well for Siena. The massive Florentine Guelph army was bolstered by additional troops sent from Arezzo, Campiglia, Colle, Lucca, Orvieto, Pistoia, Prato, Pitigliano, San Gimignano, San Miniato, and Volterra. The Sienese Ghibbeline army was much smaller, and supported only by its German and Pisan allies, some soldiers from Cortona, and a bunch of mercenaries, for a total of 17,000 troops.

The atmosphere in Siena became very tense. The citizens flocked to the Duomo to pray for protection. They formed long processions in which they stripped off their shirts and shoes and with bowed heads implored the Madonna to intercede on their behalf. The entire city rang with "Te Deums"; bishops preached to thousands of terrorized, genuflecting Sienese with tears in their eyes. During a famous ceremony a bishop handed over the keys of the city to the Virgin, with the words, "Glorious queen of the skies, I donate to you this city and beg you protect it and free it from the hands of those infamous Florentines. Liberate us from those lions that come to devour us."

On September 4, 1260, the Sienese decided to take the first step and launch a surprise attack on the Florentines, who had moved their troops to Monteaperti—just 3 miles southeast of Siena (though recent studies doubt that location and believe that the battle was actually fought at Pievasciata). The Sienese paraded their troops before the hill, then changed direction and paraded a second time, then changed again and paraded a third time, fooling the Florentines into thinking the Sienese forces were three times larger than the reality.

The battle commenced when the second Ghibbeline division, commanded by Giordano d'Angiano, attacked the right flank of the Guelph army. The clash was by all accounts devastating. Then Aldobrandino Aldobrandeschi, commander of the third division, charged through the center. The two infantries battled on the hill of Monselvoli.

Apart from being more numerous, the Guelph army also had the advantage of being placed in a better position, overlooking the enemy from the top of the hill. And indeed despite their courage the Ghibbelines seemed to be once again succumbing to the might of the Guelphs when suddenly the fourth division of cavaliers, commanded by Niccolò Bigozzi, attacked from the left flank.

The battle degenerated into a bloodbath, and the valley was filled with the fallen; screams of the injured cut through the din ofwarfare. The Sienese lost two of their most charismatic commanders, Ugurgeri and Beccarini. At great risk, some women from Siena entered the fields to help the injured and bring food.

Then at 6:00 P.M. the count of Arras arrived with his 400 fresh horsemen, and the battle cry of San Giorgio resounded across the valley. The Florentines, blinded by the setting sun, were massacred in what must have been a heartrending scene.

After eleven hours of ceaseless fighting, the Guelphs lost their left flank and fled, leaving behind on the battlefield some 20,000 dead; Siena, outnumbered at the start, had won the day.

On the morning of September 5, the Sienese returned home. One of the Florentine ambassadors who had, just days before, threatened that the city would be razed, traveled with them as a prisoner, tied to the back of a donkey and led through the city gate dragging the Florentine flag behind him. Behind him Aldobrandino Aldobrandeschi, Provenzan Salvani, and all the other victorious generals marched between two flanks of cheering citizens. The soldiers had crowned their heads with olive branches.

Many Florentines now fled to nearby Lucca and Bologna, fearing that the Sienese would press their advantage and pillage and destroy their unarmed city; but for some reason this did not occur. Just a few years later, Florence managed to rally and reorganize, and in 1269 the two armies clashed again in Colle Val d'Elsa. This time it was the Sienese who tasted defeat, and Provenzan Salvani, one of the heroes of Monteaperti, was killed.

As I stand on the site, I imagine what the placid field before me must have looked like after the battle, strewn as it was with thousands of corpses, left to rot in the mud—an incredible waste of young human lives in a cause now completely irrelevant. For a moment the sheer, mad folly of war—anywhere, at any time—overwhelms me; then a car zips by on the empty road leading to my village, and spotting the Florentine license plate I reflexively say to myself, "*Remember Monteaperti!*"

12:34 P.M.

For some time I can't tear my eyes from the battlefield. My meditation on Monteaperti's tragic epilogue has so altered my mood that I expect to look up and find the sky turned dramatically black, lightning flashing across it like filigree, then yawning open to unleash a heavy hailstorm to send me scurrying for shelter. But when I do lift my eyes, all above me is still intensely blue; the swallows are still diving joyfully into the valley, and the lizards sunning on the rocks. As if to mock my expectations, a light breeze skirts me, gently tugging my collar, then moving on to stir young green blades of grain in the adjacent field.

I think about how the mind plays tricks on itself. Even so, there are other visions and apparitions associated with Monteaperti that aren't so easily explained away . . .

Full-Moon Stories

Monteaperti inevitably left behind its trails of legends. Since the fifteenth century there have been reports of ghosts on the empty battlefield, clearly seen by eyewitnesses, roaming around under the full moon as if lost. Even today few people care to visit the site at night.

Often, on the anniversary of the battle, huge storms break out over the site, and what appear to be thousands of white cloths move across it as if tossed by the winds. A more common phenomenon of Monteaperti is the recurring noise of the battle, the cries and the laments of the dying soldiers pleading desperately for help.

Recently some tourists, unaware of the legend, passed the spot in their rental car late at night. Close to the hill they came across a cavalier riding a white horse. Because he was barring their way, they warily got out of the car and confronted him; they stared at each other for a few moments, then he galloped off, vanishing in the distance—but leaving no hoofprints behind.

Another encounter involved some locals out for a country stroll. Suddenly the wind kicked up with ferocious force, followed by the noise of drums, which grew louder with each beat. A thick fog arose, whipped by the winds, making it impossible to see for more than 50 yards; and just beyond that range came the sounds of horses' hooves and deafening human laments. About twenty minutes later the wind died down, the fog melted away, and the mysterious noises abated.

Chianti is full of stories and legends of this kind. We have our share of ghosts, werewolves, and other mythical beasts. Vampire stories were once rife in the countryside. Farmers feared the cypress tree, which they believed was a favorite gathering spot for these creatures. Even today the landscape is dotted with wooden crosses raised to keep them away. The belief was that vampires rose from the local cemeteries, and that they were the bodies of the rich nobles returned to molest the farmers in death as they had in life.

One of the most famous vampires operated very close to my village—specifically on the white road that leads to Pianella. One morning in the nineteenth century, a local butcher found large chunks of meat missing from his shop. At first he thought it was a prank played on him by his friends, but when the same thing happened another night, he began to suspect that a starving wild animal had found some way to enter the shop. That night he kept vigil outside, in the shadows, to see if he could catch the intruder. And his blood ran cold when he saw the shop's former proprietor, who had died years before, enter. The butcher crept up to the window and peered inside, where he witnessed his predecessor devouring raw meat directly from the carcasses hanging upside down on the iron hooks, his face streaming with blood. The scales in the shop were all spinning crazily and the shelves trembling. Terrified, the butcher fled the scene, and days later sold the shop for a ridiculously low price.

In 1337 two antagonistic noble families, the Salimbeni and Tolomei, agreed to a peaceful meeting near Montapearti to settle their disputes. After an abundant lunch and many liters of wine, the oldest member of the Salimbeni clan pronounced the phrase, "Now, my beloved, each one take his," which was the signal for the members of his family to leap into action. They drew hidden knives, attacking their unarmed guests and brutally massacring them one by one. Since that day many people report hearing both the sounds of the cutlery and the laments of the dying Tolomei coming from that hill, now called Malamerenda (Bad Snack).

Farther afield, we can hear similar stories. At the monastery of Coltibuono, legend has it that a group of headless monks roam the surrounding forests in procession, singing religious hymns (a mean feat, given that they have no heads). Apparently they are harmless and simply ignore anyone who sees them. Then there is the legend of a beast, half fish and half ox, that guards a treasure left by the Etruscans in an underwater cave in a nearby river; it meows when approached by humans.

Perhaps the most famous ghost, however, is that of the Baron Ricasoli. He owned the impressive Castle Brolio to which I escort many of my clients, and which has been the theater of many bitter battles over the centuries. Today it is inhabited by the same family that built it 1,000 years ago. The baron is their most famous ancestor; in 1861 he was the Italian prime minister, and was also the inventor of Chianti wine. In his time he was known as the Iron Baron due to his despotic attitude, and the fact that his ghost is still widely believed to be around is evidence that farmers are still in some way terrified by this long-dead landowner.

On the other side of the valley lies a lake that people once believed was inhabited by a large prehistoric reptile—a kind of Tuscan version of the Loch Ness monster. It would drag into its dark waters any unfortunate fisherman it snatched from the banks.

Monte Amiata, the final boundary of the Sienese territory that rises imperiously in my southern view, has its own ghost stories. There is the tale of two lovers who, because they were from vastly different social classes, were forced to meet secretly. When they were finally discovered, the young countess was forced by her family to wed a nobleman; and now, even after many centuries, on the first night of summer a female figure with a white cape is seen descending into the forest at a slow pace, her feet never quite touching the ground. There she meets her lost lover under a beech tree. Sometimes, though, he isn't there to meet her, and it's possible to hear her weeping softly well into the night.

On the road that leads to that mountain—legend tells—lives a very nasty spirit who scares anyone who happens to encroach on his turf. He appears at first very small, but as he approaches his eyes light up and suddenly his dimensions triple, so that he blocks out the setting sun.

In those same forests people swear to have met an old man wandering at night, holding a small torch that emits a green light over his pale, cadaverous face. Apparently he was the owner of a nearby castle that was destroyed in the Middle Ages, and which he now seeks endlessly, in vain.

My eyes again focus on my village right below me, with its stone houses attached to the church. Who knows how many stories of spirits and ghosts have been told around the crackling flames of its hearths, or in the dim candlelight before electricity arrived to dispel the shadows of winter nights?

Though electricity is no impediment to the most stubborn spirits. There is a small tower just a few miles away that the locals say was built by a nobleman as a trysting place for him and his lover, a young peasant girl. When his wife discovered the affair, she went to the tower and strangled her rival to death. The current owners of the house have never encountered the victim's ghost, but they've told me that often their guests, who are unaware of the story, will greet them at breakfast by saying, "Who was the young girl I saw sleeping on the couch when I got up for a glass of water last night?"

1:41 P.M.

I feel a hand on my shoulder and jump. "*Scusa,* Dario, I didn't mean to scare you." I turn and recognize Lidia, an old woman who each day comes this way to pay respects to her husband, buried in a cemetery close by. Although he died two decades ago, she faithfully brings fresh flowers on each visit, and polishes the green marble headstone with a cloth. Her dedication is extraordinary, and so is her determination: Her age doesn't prevent her from climbing the steep hill.

She always wears a black dress and blouse, and her expression is very sad. She lives alone in a small, ancient house composed of two rooms in the center of the village. She gazes at me now with even more poignancy in her look. "I heard about Cristina," she says in a near whisper. "I'm sorry."

"*Grazie, Lidia,*" I reply; "it will be hard to recover."

"You will, you will, you are so young." After a pause, she adds, "When are you going to start working again?"

I shrug. "I'm thinking of taking some time off. I need it."

She nods in approval, then pats my shoulder, says, "*Addio, Dario,*" and continues on her trek to the cemetery.

I find myself thinking about the coming year. It seems I'm

going to have quite a bit of time for myself, unlike previous seasons when I was overwhelmed by work. I stand up and head down the path, thinking about the last time I had a few days off in the middle of my tourist high season . . .

A Few Days Off

I had worked for something like thirty-five days without a break, and for this reason I was very happy to rise one morning with the sure knowledge that I had two whole days to myself. Not that I disliked my job—on the contrary, meeting new people each day and showing them the places I love is extremely rewarding, especially considering that the majority of my guests are so receptive, listening attentively and soaking up all I tell them about the area's history, art, and natural beauties. As pleasurable as it undeniably is, though, it's still a job, and like all jobs requires a rest every now and then.

I let myself sleep in for a while, and when I got out of bed Cristina had already left home for her own job and office. I lazily contemplated the hills from the bedroom window, sipping a cup of tea. It was a nice, warm June morning; the views were perfectly clear, with no sign of that unattractive heat haze that ruin the vistas when the temperature starts climbing in July and August. I decided to go to Siena for a workout in the gym, then later return to fetch my dog Pixyprozac (The dog's name was Pixy, then Cristina added Prozac because of the dog's rather sad, depressed character.) and go for a swim in the creek.

After a couple of hours working up a hard sweat—necessary to eliminate the many liters of wine I had drained over the previous days—I relaxed in the sauna and took a long shower. I left the gym feeling refreshed and invigorated. All I needed now to complete my program was a nice, cold swim.

When I reached the parking lot, however, I couldn't find my little red mini van anywhere. It wasn't where I had left it, and though I turned slowly and scanned in all directions, there was no sign of it. It was gone.

I felt the first stirrings of panic, and tried to quell them by acting in a practical manner. I returned to the gym, hoping to find my friends giggling at having played such a fine joke on me; but by the concerned look on their faces when I told them what had happened, I realized they had no clue what I was talking about. Giving in to panic, I threw my duffel bag on the floor and sank into the couch, burying my face in my hands as cold beads of sweat rolled down my forehead.

Siena is a city with a very low crime rate, and for me it had become a habit simply to leave the keys in the ignition. I had never even thought about insurance. If someone had now taken my van, I had no recourse, and no one to blame but myself.

My companions tried to comfort me and urged me to go immediately to the police station to report the theft. I took their advice, racing frenetically to the old town, through the stone gate at Porta Ovile, then scurrying up the steep Via Vallerozzi and making my way as determinedly as possibly down the main street through the Piazza del Campo—now full of busloads of tourists scattered on the cobblestones, taking in the warm sun and making the medieval square look more like a crowded beach along the Italian Riviera than the elegant cultural center of the city.

The police headquarters is right next to the Duomo, and even here I was forced to make my way through hundreds of tourists immortalizing with their cameras and video recorders the splendid cathedral, symbol of the ambitious Sienese republic. Fortunately, given the state I was in by the time I reached him, the desk officer was very helpful, promising that the police would do everything they could to find my car. He had me fill out a few forms, then told me in a reassuring tone that as soon as they had news they would summon me.

Back on the street I felt so desperate that I even considered entering the cathedral and lighting a candle, despite not being a worshipper. But the sight of the long line at the entrance put me off that idea, and I decided instead to stop for a sandwich at the wine bar just down the road.

Bruno the bartender noticed something wrong in my expression and asked if everything was *a posto*. I gushed forth my recent misadventure and the trouble I was in: I had to get a new van immediately, because in just two days I was to pick up some clients for a country tour.

"They stole my car this morning, too," interjected a raucous voice from the far end of the bar. It belonged to an extreme right-winger nicknamed "Fuehrer," a notorious troublemaker whom we all consequently avoided.

As he approached us, I noticed he was wearing a green military jacket with swastikas and skulls stitched onto the sleeves. "I just reported the theft," he continued, "but if I get hold of the bastard before the police do, his days are numbered." He rubbed his goatee menacingly with his left hand.

"Where did it happen, and what time?" I asked.

"Around nine thirty, in front of the train station. Why?"

"Hm," I replied, something coming together in my head. "I think I know where your car might be. Let's go." I motioned him to follow me while I slipped off my stool, sliding some change over to Bruno.

The neo-Nazi followed me out of the bar and into the streets, and without saying a word we threaded our way through the horde of tourists taking in the city at their maddeningly relaxed pace. We walked all the way back to the gym. As I'd guessed, his black Volkswagen Beetle convertible was exactly where I had imagined, right next to the spot where I'd left my own vehicle hours earlier.

Fuehrer ran to his car, flung open the door, and without thanking me—or even saying good-bye—lurched into motion and zoomed off at full speed. Even so, I was proud of my deduction that the car thief had abandoned Fuehrer's battered Beetle to take my van. Still, my situation hadn't changed; I was still at square one.

I called a taxi and asked to be taken to the local Subaru dealer. On arrival I told him my story, and while I believe he really did feel sorry for me, I also knew that he must have been rubbing his hands in anticipation.

While he was showing me a brand-new model, his cell phone rang. "Yep," he said, "Subaru car dealer here . . . what? . . . Yes, yes, he's here . . . Oh, yes? Where? . . . Fine, I'll tell him."

Flipping his phone shut, he said, "Relax, Dario, that was the Opel dealer. Apparently they have your car in Poggibonsi. You can go and fetch it." I felt like hugging him. Instead I ran to the station pumping my arms in the air as if I had just scored the win for Italy in the World Cup final, and hopped the first train to Poggibonsi.

When I reached the small, drab industrial town, a few miles north of Siena, I took another cab and had the driver leave me at the address the Subaru dealer had given me. I immediately spotted my van parked inside the fenced yard of the Opel dealership.

I introduced myself to the owner, who had a horrible, hairy

birthmark that looked like a piece of wild boar fur stuck on his cheek. He explained that someone, just hours before, had stolen a brand-new Opel Corsa, still without a license plate, and had left my van in exchange.

To my delight the van was in perfect shape, nothing seemed missing but a few liters of gas. I thanked the perplexed gentleman and told him not to worry about his car: Judging by recent events, it would probably materialize somewhere very shortly, as the thief continued trading up.

On the drive back home, I couldn't help thinking about the phantom thief and trying to figure out what game he was playing. Still, the thing that really mattered was that I had regained possession of my van, so I resolved not to worry about it any longer and instead decide what to do with my next day off . . . given that the first was nearly over and almost completely ruined. All I could do to salvage it was go home and enjoy the sunset with Cristina.

We chose to watch it from the monument above the village of Vagliagli. We sat on the grass, opened a bottle of Prosecco, and while the sun slipped gloriously behind the hills I leaned over and kissed her sweetly.

The following morning was as glorious as the last. I decided to walk to the village for breakfast, then pick up Pixyprozac and a book and go directly to the *tombolotti,* where I could finally claim my swim.

Along the way I said *buongiomo* to several neighbors, including Clara, a senior lady who despite her years was proudly showing off the red hat she'd purchased at the market the day before.

I sat outside a nearby cafe, ordered a whole wheat honey bun and barley coffee, and—because I'm a typical Italian—started leafing through the pink daily Italian sports paper, the legendary *Gazzetta dello Sport,* the biggest-selling daily newspaper in Italy. Its reporting was so thorough that today more than twenty-eight of its forty pages focused on the Italian Soccer League, despite the season being over.

I then picked up the local *Corriere di Siena,* and on the front page, in huge type, was a headline that caught my eye:

CAR THIEF CAPTURED ON THE SIENA–GROSSETO ROAD

> In a brilliant operation yesterday the local *carabinieri* arrested Giorgio Soru, aged 48, at 9:00 P.M. Signor Soru, a man with psychological problems, had been allowed a 48-hour release permit from the clinic where he was being held. It was during his release, the *carabinieri* reported, that he stole a moped belonging to Francesca Butini, a nurse employed by the clinic. He abandoned the scooter in Via Fiorentina and picked up a Volkswagen Beetle, which he consequently left at the Presidents Gym Health Club's private parking lot, exchanging it for a red Subaru four-wheel-drive mini van. The van was found hours later in Poggibonsi, where Soru stole a brand-new Opel Corsa, which he drove to Colle Val d'Elsa, abandoning it in turn in Piazza Arnolfo. Investigators report that here Soru took possession of a Class A Mercedes, which, on his return to Siena, he swapped at a Coop supermarket for a truck that had just finished unloading some frozen goods. The driver, Signor Giovanni Francini, was in the supermarket's office signing the delivery papers,

and didn't realize his truck had been taken till he returned and found it gone. Apparently no one saw Soru leaving the warehouse premises.

In Viale Sardegna the thief approached Mrs. Paola Fanti, who reported that he rolled down the truck's window and assaulted her with a stream of obscene phrases before zooming off at full speed, heading south. Despite the shock of the encounter, Signora Fanti was sufficiently quick witted to memorize the license plate and call the *carabinieri*.

Soru was arrested that evening close to Fontazzi on the Siena–Grosseto state road; apparently he was trying to convince a prostitute to exchange her company for a carton of frozen runner beans. On the arrival of the *carabinieri*, Soru offered no resistance and was escorted to the local jail. Soru is reportedly not new to these types of pranks.

The *maresciallo* of the *carabinieri* pointed out that all the vehicles Soru stole yesterday had the keys in the ignition, and invites citizens to refrain from this bad habit.

I laughed out loud as I read this, disturbing a couple of German tourists seated at the table behind me, and kept giggling all the way home.

The sky was an intense and inviting blue, not a single cloud to be seen, and the uncultivated field in front of my house was dotted with thousands of red poppies, standing perfectly still in the total absence of wind.

I packed my duffel bag with a towel, a book, a bottle of red wine, and a few slices of *bresaola*—but no swimsuit. Today, I thought, nakedness and no cell phone were the thing. Utter freedom! I slipped a leash around Pixyprozac's neck . . . but just as I was closing the door behind me the phone on the coffee table rang.

It was Nino, a concierge at one of the most prestigious hotels in the area. "*Ciao, Dario,*" he said. "Did you see the paper?"

"*Si, Nino,*" I replied, perplexed. "But how did you know it was my car they were writing about? They didn't use my name."

"You're the only idiot in the whole of Tuscany with a red four-by-four Subaru mini van. Who else could buy such an ugly heap?"

"Listen, Nino, if you've called to laugh at me, forget it. Today's my day off, and I'm just off for a swim."

"*Perfetto, Dario!* You're free, then, and you've saved my life. See, when I asked if you'd read the paper, I was actually talking about the article *below* the one about the car theft—the one that mentions the American senator visiting Siena."

"So?" I replied, suddenly wary.

"Well, you see, he's booked a suite right here, and he's traveling with his secretary and his ten-year-old son. And today the senator and his secretary had to leave urgently for Rome, but the babysitter's just taken ill and the two boys have to be entertained for the day, and was thinking that you might—"

"No, no," I interrupted, "it's my day off and I don't want to be disturbed. And anyway you said first there's only one son—now you say two. What gives?"

"The other is the secretary's son, same age. The senator thought it was a good idea to bring him along, to keep his boy company. They're very good kids. Dario, come on, help me out, I can't find anyone but you."

"Nino, *no,*" I said as firmly as possible. "That's final. And you know me, when I say no, I *mean* no."

Twenty minutes later I was driving toward the five-star lodging, flinging imprecations to the winds. I parked the van outside the main entrance (this time pausing to take the keys from the ignition) and found Nino waiting for me dressed in a tuxedo, looking at this hour ridiculous, like a penguin.

"Dario," he said, "couldn't you at least have worn a tie?"—but his criticism was offset by the arm he swung around my neck to pat me on the shoulder. "Come on, I'll introduce you to the kids. All you have to do is take them to Castle Meleto and show them a wine cellar, then a quick lunch and be back by four. Okay?"

Inside, he left me in the lounge and dashed back behind the hardwood reception desk to answer a phone call. Seated on the couch were the two little boys. One of them stood up to greet me; he wore a pair of gray shorts, a white shirt, a navy-blue tie, and a pair of polished black lace-up shoes. Perched on his nose was a pair of thick reading glasses that he removed and polished while looking up toward me. "Mr. Castagno, I presume," he said. "I read your book, I thought it was appalling." He clasped my hand perfunctorily and told me his name was Edmonton.

"I'm Steve," said the other boy, with a big grin splayed across his freckled face. His carrot-red hair was covered by a baseball cap; he wore a pair of low-waist baggy jeans with his underwear sticking out the top, right over a snow-white belly that was only partly covered by a pop-band T-shirt. He gave me a high five and said, "Let's go!"

As I took them to the car, I thought what an odd couple they were; one couldn't have been more different from the other. Steve sat next to me in front and asked me many questions; Edmonton slouched in the backseat and sulked for the entire drive to Meleto.

At both stops Steve was curious to learn the history of the castle, and in the cellars was keen to hear the secrets of wine-making. Edmonton spoke only to announce that his house was larger than the castle, and better because it was newer, and that his family never drank Italian wines because French Bordeaux were far superior.

At lunch Edmonton couldn't find anything to satisfy him. When I asked him his favorite dish, he flabbergasted me by replying, "Foie gras," which he was annoyed to find missing from the menu. Thanks only to Steve's smooth persuasion, he finally agreed to order a plate of pasta. On the drive back I noticed that despite being worlds apart the boys somehow got along well together. Steve had a clearly beneficial influence on Edmonton, and I must admit that he saved me several times during the day.

When we returned to the hotel, I saw a big black limousine parked outside and realized that the senator had returned. In fact, in the entrance hall I was greeted by a large, friendly gentleman who asked if his son had had a good time and behaved well. "Yes, he had a great time," I lied; then, to my amazement, it became clear that I hadn't when Steve ran into his arms exclaiming, "Hey, Dad!"

On the way back home I recalled the Italian proverb *L'abito non fa il monaco*—the clothes don't make the monk. Or, apparently, the senator's son. A fit lesson for the day; which, coupled with yesterday's lesson regarding car keys, gave me two learning experiences in two days. Not quite the vacation I'd hoped for, but in the end good enough.

2:06 P.M.

I walk past a bush of Spanish broom, its flowers bright yellow, and catch a whiff of its sweet fragrance. As I stoop to breathe in even more of it, a *poccione* sucker snake is spooked by my shadow and disappears into a tiny crack in the rock. I'm amazed that such a large reptile can fit through such a narrow opening; leaning in, I can see its long green body coiled up inside the dusty sanctuary. The locals believe that this snake is particularly fond of milk, and that it sneaks into the stables to suckle cows' udders—even that it is attracted to nursing women. It isn't the most feared snakes in these hills—it's not poisonous like the viper—but unlike the viper it can be very aggressive. I had a bad experience years ago when, while picking mushrooms in the forest, I accidentally disturbed a couple of snakes copulating. They reared up and then came darting at me. Utterly terrified, I fled through the thick vegetation, scratching my face and ripping my shirt on the blackberry bushes, until I found my way out.

The wind now changes direction and suddenly the air is filled with white smoke coming from a nearby olive grove. It's old Cesarino, burning the olive branches he's been pruning. He's too far away to spot me and I have no desire to disturb him, as he's not a very talkative man. A tiny fellow, he is famous in the village for wearing jeans that are several sizes too large and then cinching them up around his armpits.

I turn away from Cesarino, confident he knows what he's doing. In fact, forest fires are uncommon in these hills, which are well patrolled. Yet even though my eyes now roam elsewhere, the scent of the burning leaves stays with me and fills my lungs. It brings back memories of my time as a firefighter . . .

Dario the Fireman

When I was a teenager, I lived with my parents outside Castellina in Chianti, a village some 15 miles north of Siena inhabited by approximately 2,000 souls. I spent most of my spare time with my small group of friends, roaming across the Chianti hills on our motorbikes or hiking through the oak forests, exploring the hundreds of abandoned farmhouses—a passion to which I dedicated a few chapters of my last book. Happiness for us was to bathe in crystal-clear creek waters, or to sit on the hilltops contemplating the endless views and listening to psychedelic music, smoking our homegrown grass, cultivated illegally in our secret spots along the rivers. We would exchange books written by authors from the Beat Generation, recite poems, and read underground magazines. We tuned in to the radio stations that broadcast from private homes, which were very much in vogue in those years, and to make ourselves even cooler we deliberately adopted pronounced Tuscan accents. We let our hair grow long and then dyed it, and we were the first generation of village men to pierce our ears. We formed rock bands and rehearsed in old barns. We felt *very* alternative, and weren't at all interested in the commercial teen icons or fashions of that era.

The majority of us came from simple backgrounds; most of my friends' parents were farmers or laborers employed by the local flour mill. They were the generation that had survived the war; some were illiterate, and few had ever crossed the Tuscan borders. They had passed most of their existences breaking their backs trying to get something from the rocky Chianti soil. Yet despite all this they had no trouble accepting our hippie lifestyles; in this way they were curiously more sophisticated and open minded than many of their more educated and wider-traveled contemporaries in the larger cities.

What we had in common with our parents was a deep attachment to the land. We were indifferent to the bustling cities most youngsters longed to move to; our sole desire was to remain in our beloved Chianti. All we needed was an isolated, abandoned farmhouse, a fireplace, a *fiasco* of wine, and some sausages to roast on the glowing embers in good company. We were content with such simplicity.

But life wasn't all a rustic idyll. Something all youngsters dreaded at that time was the day we would receive the *cartolina*—the postcard that called us to mandatory military service for a year. It was an inevitability that we knew would completely change our lives for twelve months. Even worse, it would remove us from our cherished home grounds.

I was only seventeen at the time, and life for me was simply a game. Even the idea of donating one of the best years of my life to the Italian state didn't bother me too much, despite the many stories I'd heard of the inhuman treatment our older friends had experienced during their terms—which, I was convinced, they exaggerated to scare us. Still, it was disheartening to see some of our older friends, whose laid-back counterculture glamour we'd all tried to emulate, return from their year of duty transformed—suddenly clean shaven, with crew cuts, looking and acting like normal, unremarkable grown-ups.

One afternoon I returned home from work, and as I parked my motorbike in the garage I saw my mother on the doorstep, waving a yellow *cartolina* at me. My heart sank; I had always known it was just a matter of time, but even so, I slapped my forehead in frustration and grief.

I took the postcard from my mother. On the front it read ITALIAN MINISTRY OF DEFENSE. I opened it slowly and read that the following week I was to show up at the Caserma Cavalli in Florence for my physical.

That winter was one of the coldest of the century. Most of the olive trees died and had to be cut down. The day I went to Florence there was a fierce blizzard, and I felt the wind like a knife as I crossed over the River Arno on foot, something I had never done before. Shivering, I stood in a long line in front of the barracks.

During the wait I recognized a couple of friends from a nearby village, both wearing the same defeated look; they were an inseparable duo known for modifying the engines of their Vespas—and for breaking many teenage girls' hearts. Paolo, who was wrapped up in leather, gave me a friendly hug. "Nabbed you, too, eh?" he said. "How did you get here?" I explained that I had come by rail, and that despite the storm and the frozen tracks my train had had somehow managed to reach its destination.

"And you?" I asked. Giulio jerked his thumb toward a pair of Vespas parked alongside the road, the smirk in his face showing that he knew he'd just revealed something extraordinary.

And indeed I was impressed: They'd driven 40 miles to Florence on frozen roads, risking their necks at every ice-slicked turn.

"We've decided not to do military service," they then explained proudly. I asked how this was possible. In a conspiratorial whisper, Paolo said, "We've looked into a few systems."

Finally the large wooden door creaked open and the whole scruffy lot of us was allowed to swarm into the well-heated building. There we were subjected to blood and urine tests, heart exams, and a brief interview. Finally, after a ridiculous written questionnaire, we were free to go.

On the way out I saw Giulio, who triumphantly waved a paper in my face. He had been excused duty! As my jaw dropped in awe, he explained that he'd pretended to be deaf and had succeeded in fooling the doctors. A sergeant even rang a cow bell close to his ear, but he'd managed not to wince.

While we descended the stairs to the exit, I was about to ask what happened to Paolo when we heard a large coin drop behind us. Giulio instinctively turned around to collect it, and saw the sergeant at the top of the staircase. The angry military man's voice resounded through the cavernous hall. "*Figlio di troia*," he bellowed, "*sei fottuto uto!*" You son of a bitch—you're finished!

Giulio realized he was in big trouble now. He gave me a farewell look, his eyes brimming with angry tears, then lowered his head and climbed slowly back toward the sergeant, who ordered him immediately to his office.

Poor Giulio was enrolled in the Grenadiers and sent to a barracks known laughingly as Fort Apache, located in a no-man's-land in the mountains of Sardinia—considered the worst possible place for a term of duty, and in fact reserved by the army as a punishment destination. Curiously, he spent the entire year there with Paolo, who'd ended up on the island for a very different reason. During his interview, one of the questions asked by the sergeant was, "Have you ever had sexual intercourse?" Paolo, for motives unknown even to himself, chose to answer: "Does it count if it was with your wife?"

Back home I ran into another friend of mine, Enzo, who'd carried out his own plan to avoid military service: When he received his postcard, he had hopped on his Vespa and ridden all the way to Orvieto, in Umbria, where there is a famous wishing well, *il pozzo di San Patrizio.* According to tradition, if you throw a coin into the well, you will be granted one wish. Enzo wished not to be called up for the service. He smiled as he told me this, pleased with his ingenuity and confident that his wish would come true. Later on, of course, I heard that not only was Enzo called to duty, but he was stationed . . . in Orvieto!

In reality, during those years the only sure way to escape military service was to declare during the interview that you were totally against any form of violence and the use of weapons; in this case you were dismissed from military service but still had to work in a public service capacity. It was certainly a much better choice, allowing the chance to help people in need. The catch was that the term of service was three years, and to be honest that was far too much for me. I was already working, out of necessity, and the idea of not receiving any wages for so long was out of the question.

There was, however, a way to pass the year in a military force where the discipline was mild, the training good fun, and you were taught things that might actually be useful in the future. The fire brigade! Add in the facts that after two months of training you were sent to a billet close to your hometown, and that the food in the stations was known to be excellent, and it was a perfect alternative. Of course, almost everyone volunteered to join this force, so the odds against being selected were enormous; only 1 in 10,000 managed to get in. But I was determined to be that very one.

In that period I was single, and apart from some one-day adventures I had never really had any steady relationships. I now started dating a young woman called Sabina whom I'd known casually for years. I'd always known that she was interested in me, given the way her face turned red each time I said hello, and the way she constantly kept her eyes on me. She was a kind person, full of life, with long, dark hair and beautiful chestnut eyes. She had one weird habit, though: Whenever she found herself in a place that required respectful silence, she couldn't help bursting into laughter. While visiting a church, a museum, or even a hospital in her company, I often found myself in embarrassing situations.

Nevertheless, I was fond of her. She was slim enough to have no problems fitting on the back of my motorbike. We took many cross-country jaunts, sometimes even going to the beaches. She was so trusting, however, that she would actually fall asleep in the saddle, and the only way to keep her slipping off altogether was to tie her firmly to my waist with a rope.

We started seeing each other almost every day, and I realized with surprise that I was developing strong feelings for her. One day we decided to go to our favorite spot, a cypress forest perched atop a hill. To reach this beautiful place, we had to ride over a number of muddy fields and climb a path so narrow and rocky that I often had to ground a foot to avoid plummeting into the volcanic crags below.

Sabina had prepared a picnic basket that we'd tied behind the bike, and when we reached the spot she laid out a plaid blanket on the moss. We settled ourselves on the blanket, ravenous, and wolfed down the sandwiches and wine she had brought.

While we admired the setting sun, embracing, I gently told her that very soon I would be called away for my military service, as I had passed the physical and was waiting for my final assignment. I explained that I had no connections of any kind and that for this reason I would almost certainly be posted far away, possibly Sicily or, worse, some desolate place in the Dolomite Mountains to guard some stupid ammunition depot over endless ice-cold nights. Sabina listened in silence, tears rolling down her cheeks. Then she gazed up at me with her deep brown eyes and said that she couldn't live a whole year apart from me. She told me that her father was the fire chief in Siena, and that if she asked him, with a bit of luck he could have me put on the rolls.

"Really?" I said—pretending not to know what her father's occupation was; not, in fact, to have known all along. I hugged her and told her that if she could do this for me, I would be in her debt for the rest of my life.

A couple of months later, while doffing my crash helmet in the garage, I was again met by my mother with a *cartolina*. I opened this one slowly and saw what I was hoping for: "Dario Castagno—Fire Brigade School of Rome." I had made it!

I immediately went to the local bar to meet my friends, the majority depressed—like me, they had received "the postcard." Some had been called to serve in the infantry, others with the paratroopers, still others the air force and navy. When I told them where I was going, they called me names even I hadn't heard before, and forced me to pay for the entire rounds of drinks.

Weeks later I was in Rome, and after two months of tough

training I was sent back to Siena for an easy year of hanging out at the firehouse. My feelings for Sabina perhaps inevitably waned, since it seems clear now I had more or less willed them into being. At the end of the year I broke up with her and returned to bumming around the Chianti hills, alone.

Even today, despite twenty years having passed, when I encounter Sabina with her kids she has difficulty saying hello. I doubt that she has forgiven me. In all honesty I can't blame her.

2:31 P.M.

I'm getting hungry. I pull my wallet from my back pocket and realize I have no euros, just a few stray American dollars left over from my trip. At home the refrigerator is empty, and I have no intention of asking Roberto at the local grocery store if I can shop today, pay tomorrow. He would probably allow it, but grudgingly, and I don't want to spoil my first day back with his unfriendly looks, or have my name scrawled in his black book to the tune of one of his famously unfriendly grunts.

Even so, my stomach is grumbling and needs to be appeased. I try to consider what I might do, but the hunger is making me a little light-headed. It's hard to think.

As I'm standing there wondering, a car comes screaming up the road at full speed; its front wheels hit a pothole, causing its back end to jerk suddenly and the trunk to fly open. A shopping bag bounces out onto the road. I shout out to the driver, but he disappears around a corner in a cloud of dust.

I shrug, then go to see what he's lost. It's a bag from the Coop supermarket and when I open it, I find, to my astonishment, a warm *prosciutto panino,* a plastic bottle of white wine, a stuffed focaccia, some fresh fruit, and a cream bun. I can't believe my luck.

I stand by the roadside for a few minutes in case the car returns for its lost cargo, but even as I do so I know it won't; wherever the driver was heading, he clearly wasn't stopping till he got there. Casting my eyes heavenward, I thank providence and sit back down. With great satisfaction, I tuck into my free lunch. While I'm chewing the salty prosciutto sandwich and taking in the view, my mind drifts back to another unexpected meal . . .

Manna from Heaven

Unlike most of my close friends, Andrea is not an old buddy I grew up with in the village, nor a companion of my teenage Chianti escapades. In fact our paths crossed as adults for the most banal of reasons: I had to take out life insurance. Because I'm firmly convinced that all such policies are the same no matter what company you choose, I ended up selecting Andrea's, because his ad in the yellow pages boasted that the office had a private parking lot. You might think that wasn't a sufficient incentive, but it saved me 10,000 lire.

The receptionist at the insurance office was wearing a very chaste suit; she led me to the director's office and, pointing toward a leather armchair, told me to make myself comfortable, Signor Andrea Giubbolini was concluding a meeting in the conference room next door and would be with me in a few minutes. I killed time looking at the company advertisements on the wall; each poster showed happy, smiling families, tall husbands with light blue eyes embracing equally tall, equally blue-eyed wives, each holding the hands of children with light blue eyes who weren't very tall yet, but give them time.

Signor Giubbolini made his appearance wearing a huge grin on his plump face. He was small and round with a ridiculous lock of long hair combed over his bald head; it started from his left temple and dangled over his right ear. Judging by the firmness with which those few stray hairs were attached to his head, I guessed that he had studiously applied a hefty quantity of gel while standing in front of the mirror. He was dressed as I imagine any chief sales coordinator employed by a big corporation would be: expensive brown leather shoes, a navy-blue Armani suit, and a tie to match.

He shook my hand energetically, and minutes later I found myself signing an insurance contract with a twenty-year expiration date, which like all the others promised a huge sum at termination—so large that you want to fast-forward ahead twenty years so you can cash the sum and spend it on a vacation somewhere exotic. When I dictated my birth date, Andrea's face lit up: "We were born on the same day! I've never met anyone else born on the same date as me, but you were even born the same year! Amazing!"

To be funny, I voiced that possibly we were also of the same sign of the zodiac. This took a moment to sink in, then he laughed out loud, stood up, and gave me a friendly slap on my back. With a reappraising look, he said, "If we were born on the same date, how come you have so much hair?" He tenderly patted his silly little lock, as though it were an ailing houseplant that might grow back.

He glanced at his big gold Rolex, and when he saw that it was almost lunchtime politely asked if I'd like to be his guest for a quick bite at the trattoria down the road. I accepted, and as he grabbed his trench coat from the rack he told his secretary to cancel all his afternoon appointments.

We walked out onto the narrow cobble streets, and when we came to the first bar he stopped and said, "*Dario, aperitivo?*" I consented, and ordered a Prosecco. Andrea gave the middle-aged bartender a serious look and asked which product he had that he had most difficulty selling. The bartender reached up to a wooden ledge and pulled down a dusty bottle that contained, as he explained it, liquor made from asparagus by an old monk. He had purchased it back in the 1970s when he had accompanied his mother to a desolate hermitage perched somewhere in the middle of the Dolomites. The bottle was still sealed, and was now really just an ornamental piece; he doubted anyone would ever really ask for it.

Both the bartender and I thought Andrea was kidding when he ordered a glass, but he was in absolute earnest. With great ceremony the bartender opened the bottle and poured him a glass of the terrible monastic brew. We watched with keen interest as Andrea raised the glass to his lips. To our surprise, he proclaimed it "Great!" as soon as the first drop had oozed past his gums. He then opened a pack of potato chips and produced from his inner jacket a tube of mayonnaise. He kept the tube in his right hand, and each time he inserted a handful of chips into his mouth he would drop his head back and squeeze the tube right over it, sending a blob of pale yellow into his gaping maw. And then he would wash down the terrible mixture with a shot of asparagus liquor, which made me want to throw up my Prosecco on the counter.

The irony was that to Andrea all this seemed quite normal. While munching his third pack of chips, he told me that I had made a very good investment: His company had made a profit of 4.8 percent that year despite the many crises strangling the stock market. When he had squeezed dry the entire tube of mayonnaise and emptied half the bottle of distilled asparagus, he wiped his mouth on his sleeve, paid the incredulous bartender, and suggested that we get moving if we were going to have lunch.

And yet we had only gone a few more blocks before he hustled me into another bar. There I watched him wolf down a tray of mixed *crostini,* a glass of vermouth, one of Campari, and a Biancosarti, all while I was slowly sipping my second Prosecco of the day. When we finally reached the little trattoria, I realized that Andrea was a regular by the familiar way he was greeted and by the table to which we were escorted, a cozy private room in the back.

The proprietor told us that the best picks of the day were, for antipasti, a wild onion flan, a mix of cold cuts, and some porcini vol au vents; for the first course a *buristo risotto,* some ravioli that had just been made, and lemon *tagliolini;* and finally, for the main course, a knuckle of veal and a stuffed *cotechino* sausage. "Sounds good to me," Andrea said, adding that he'd like to hear about the desserts later. The owner didn't even flinch; he pivoted on his heel and scurried off in the direction of the kitchen.

Now that I had broken the ice and was getting to know this bizarre character, I felt free to ask what he was thinking of ordering. He said to me, "What do you mean? We already ordered." I thought I must have missed something. I asked, "*What* did we order?" and he, looking at me as though I were a little stupid, said, "The owner's recommendations"—*all* of them. We'd ordered a ten-course meal for lunch!

When the first trays arrived at our table, Andrea realized he had forgotten to order a side dish to accompany the main courses; he made up for this by asking for a green salad. "*Mamma* says you must eat a plate of veggies every day for a healthy diet," he remarked, just moments before he ordered two liters of the house wine. The first liter was emptied halfway through the antipasti while he talked about the Dow Jones stock indicators; the second liter disappeared by the first bite of ravioli; and of the liters that followed, I lost count.

At the next round of our first courses, he changed the subject to soccer. By the first round of our second courses, he was narrating the long list of his failures with women. With his mouth full of stuffed sausage, he admitted that often he would visit the Nigerian prostitutes on the Siena–Grosseto highway. When he started to tackle the veal knuckle (with what was probably the fifth liter of wine), he told me he was actually seeking a steady relationship—but only because what he was *really* interested in was wife swapping.

He was great company, often opening his mouth wide to give forth a deafening roar of laughter—which explained why we were alone in the back room. I pretended to continue eating, though I had long since had my fill. Still, none of the trays was sent back empty, as Andrea cleared them with relish, as well as polishing up anything I left on my plate without a moment's embarrassment. I was about ready to burst and badly needed to get out into the fresh air, but Andrea insisted on ordering a "tasting" of desserts and a bottle of Passito di Pantelleria. Then, to my amazement, he asked the waiter to bring a few slices of ham because, as he explained, "You *can't* leave this trattoria without sampling a couple of slices." I declined, so Andrea ate my portion.

Finally, after a chocolate cake, an apple tart, and a *tiramisù,* we managed to get up and leave. My head was in a whirl after what was, for me, a bout of endurance eating; but Andrea, who seemed to be in perfect fettle, took my arm and led me outside, where at last we were refreshed by an ice-cold wind that jolted me out of my sluggish torpor. As we started back, I pointed out that he had not eaten the fresh salad he'd made such a point of ordering. He shrugged and said alas, he had no more room, then barked out a laugh and suggested we visit a friend who owned a small bar, where she served a special digestive she made herself.

The bar was a scruffy, dirty little place, completely empty and lit by some unattractive neon lights. Pia, the owner, looked like a character from a Fellini movie. Her hair was dyed jet black and pulled into a nest atop her head, with a large pink plastic Spanish fan perched on the top. Her face was painted with heavy, buttery makeup, her eyelashes caked in thick mascara full of little blobs. Her gigantic frame was wrapped in a black cape and her enormous breasts were comfortably resting on the counter, which seemed to warp a little under their weight. I couldn't help taking in the startling size of those mammaries. I wondered whether it was possible to find a bra of those dimensions on the open market, or whether she had to get out needle and thread and welder's torch and run them up herself.

At the sight of Andrea, she came from behind the bar and opened her arms. He embraced her, and she left a big red lipstick mark on his plump cheek. "Two of your special digestives," he called out as he liberated himself from her lethal anaconda-like grasp. She recomposed her breasts with a few quick movements of her hands, then returned behind the Formica counter and poured an indefinable brown brew into two transparent glasses. As soon as I had taken a sip, I recognized an extremely potent homemade walnut liquor. So much for a digestive—my mouth was on fire!

Andrea, however, emptied three in a clip and then took out his cell phone, which had begun ringing with an unusual Christmas carol tone.

"Okay, *Mamma*," he said, "I'll be home in a few minutes. And say, add an extra place at the table, as a friend will be joining us for dinner." Again he swung his arm around me, adjusted his lock of hair, and explained that last week his father had slain a boar. Tonight his *mamma* was cooking it, and I couldn't possibly miss her fine cuisine.

"Dinner!" I exclaimed. "You want to have *dinner*?"

"Certainly, Dario," he replied, with complete gravity. "It's almost eight, surely you don't want to go to bed with an empty stomach. Anyway, it's too late to back out now. I already said you were coming, and she'd be very offended if I turned up alone."

As I had no intention of offending anyone, I lowered my head and, in a near-comatose state, followed Andrea to his house in the *Istrice* (Porcupine) district, within the ancient walls of the city. I wasn't feeling well; the idea of another meal made me dizzy. Andrea, however, was as fresh as a rose, looking as though he had just paid a visit to the local mineral spa in Chianciano Terme.

On the way to the house he explained that he lived with his parents and his old grandmother, who rarely spoke and suffered acute flatulence . . . but not to worry because she was stone deaf and fortunately the emissions were odorless.

When we entered the house, the family was gathered in the living room attentively following a TV sitcom. Andrea whispered instructions to me to sit down on the couch and wait in silence for the break, because his family didn't miss a single episode of *Il Principe di Bel Air,* The Prince of Bel Air, which was aired every day at this time. I obeyed and soon found myself glancing around at his family. I felt like I was in a movie wax museum. Andrea's mother was the spitting image of Jane Fonda, his father of Ernest Borgnine, while his grandmother—gently pitching to and fro on her rocking chair—was the identical twin of Tina Pica, an Italian postwar actress. As soon as she noticed me, she smiled and let out a soft hiss from beneath one thigh.

It puzzled me that a sitcom, which is supposed to be funny, was being watched by this particular audience in near-religious silence, as if they were listening to a declaration of war by our president. At the end of the show, they all came suddenly to life, standing up and greeting me with friendly faces. Andrea explained that we had met just that morning in his office, and that we were born the same day and year.

Jane's face lit up. "I wonder if your parents conceived you the same day we conceived Andrea."

"It was in the back of our Fiat 500," Ernest added with a laugh. "Those were the days!"

Andrea, not at all embarrassed, roared with laughter and invited me to sit at the table because dinner was about to be served.

Ernest poured me a glass of red wine that was, he explained, produced in the tiny vineyard their family owned in Montepulciano. He said they were always happy to have Andrea's friends over for dinner and added, to my complete astonishment, that Andrea was a teetotaler and never drank. I tried to make eye contact with Andrea, but he seemed oblivious.

Dinner consisted of *crostini* with wild boar sauce, *pappardelle* with wild boar sauce, and stewed wild boar with wild boar sauce. At this point I was expecting a wild boar sauce over ice cream, but instead Ernest poured me a glass of *vin santo,* also produced in their small family vineyard. It occurred to me that if they drank these quantities daily, the vineyard couldn't be *that* small. Tina Pica had drunk more than all rest of the family put together, and during the entire meal not a word passed her lips;

but from her other end she had been extremely talkative.

I went to the bathroom and gazed at my face in the mirror. My skin was of a weird grayish green color, and I considered booking a week in a detox clinic—either that, or the insurance policy I had taken out only that morning would be cashed in by my lucky heir very soon.

I returned to the dining room, and before I could say anything, Jane and Ernest shoved a bowl at me. Its rim was decorated with little porcupines, and it was filled with trifle. I was also given a glass of grappa, fruit (of course) of the small family vineyard. Andrea saw me regard the dessert with a kind of horrified swoon, and whispered in my ear, "You can't turn it down, Babbo would be very offended."

At the end of the meal I managed to find an excuse to leave, and said my good-byes to Jane Fonda, Ernest Borgnine, and Tina Pica. Andrea accompanied me out. He apologized for not having warned me, but for some reason he had never drunk alcohol in front of his parents. I figured it didn't matter much; he seemed to drink it everywhere else.

On the walk back to my car he told me that he was going to stop in the bar to finish the asparagus liquor produced by the monk in the hermitage lost in the Dolomites. Driving myself home with more than a little difficulty on the curves, I thought, *Where on earth could I find another character like Andrea?*

2:50 P.M.

My providential lunch complete, I lie back, my back resting on the square granite base of a monument raised in memory of the locals who were killed in World War I. This marker, in turn, faces a statue dedicated to a local hero of World War II, Bruno Bonci.

I consider the ubiquity of these monuments. In some places the First World War wiped out an entire generation of young men, sons of peasants who had never even journeyed beyond their neighboring hills but were sent to fight in the wintry mountains of northern Italy. The casualties were so high that the Italian government had been ready to send fifteen-year-olds to defend our borders; fortunately the war ended before this plan could be implemented.

Most of these monuments are collective, honoring dozens of fallen soldiers. Bruno Bonci, however, rated his own statue. I don't know why; in fact, I don't know very much about him at all. He was a patriot killed in the village in 1944, but very few people are willing to tell me more than that. Just saying his name can cause an otherwise friendly villager to fall into stony silence. But for some reason, seated here and now, I become determined to crack the wall of silence around him. It's almost as though providence threw this lunch into my lap just so I would sit before his statue and find the resolve to do so.

Most of his companions have passed away, but I'm sure Cesarino can tell me quite a lot. The problem will be breaking through his reserve. A tall order, but I'm willing to give it a try.

I leave the road and descend the hill, where I find Cesarino seated beneath an oak tree, tending the small bonfire he's made of fallen branches. He's smoking a Tuscan cigar in silence, taking in the first warmth of the late spring. As usual his jeans are pulled up under his armpits, and he sports a straw hat that doesn't prevent his thinning hair, now whiter than ever, from tumbling down over his skinny shoulders.

I sit down next to him, my presence provoking not even a flicker of acknowledgment. He stares straight ahead with his surprisingly clear blue eyes and continues to poke at his fire.

"Cesarino," I say, "how you doing?"

He turns his head slowly and says, "*Bene, Dario.*" I wait for more, but hear only the crackle of the flame. This is par for the course for Cesarino; his deep-rooted reticence makes him reluctant to say more than is absolutely necessary. But I'm determined that he'll speak at length today.

"So, Cesarino, what can you tell me about Bruno Bonci?" I ask boldly, deciding a direct question might catch him off guard.

He looks momentarily surprised, then shrugs his scrawny shoulders and with a deep breath says, "What do you want, Dario?"

"I want to know something about Bruno Bonci. I know you must have known him. I don't ask too many details, just the basics."

After a long, contemplative pause, Cesarino hauls up his crooked body and goes over to an olive tree, from whose branches he produces a sack containing a *fiasco* of red wine and two small glasses.

He sits down again and says, "Dario, have a drink and leave me alone. I know nothing about Caravaggio."

"*Caravaggio?*" I reply, leaping on his unintended revelation. "They called him Caravaggio? . . . Why?"

He sits in silence for a few minutes, pulling the cork from the bottle and filling the two glasses. The sun is very warm—I wonder at the purpose of his bonfire, but one question at a time—and a languid haze drifts over the valleys, giving them a touch of extra magic.

Cesarino looks directly into my eyes, then takes off his hat and passes his right hand through his limp hair. "I will tell you the story once," he says, "if you promise never to ask me again." He picks up his pitchfork, adds some branches to the fire, produces another cigar, bites off the tip, and lights it from one of the embers.

He takes his first puff.

And then he talks . . .

Bruno Bonci, aka Caravaggio

"In 1944 Bruno and Enzo were painting frescoes in a hall in the University of Siena when suddenly Bruno put down his paintbrush and said, 'I'm painting, yes, but what am I painting for?' Enzo did not understand. Bruno explained that in the spring he had anxious, floating sensations and found it hard to concentrate. Enzo still did not understand, but he said, 'Please continue, Bruno, I am listening.'

"'The winds of freedom have been released, Enzo. They are blowing in the hills, where they are fighting. So what are we doing here?' He was caught up in the stirring times. He said, 'I feel changed, I no longer have my feet on the ground.'

"Bruno was a generous boy, always ready to help someone in need. And he was very capable. Tall, strong, the body of an athlete. His face was a perfect oval. Large eyes, a full, expressive lower lip, in fact a mouth that seemed sculpted by an expert hand. His father would boast about his Greek statue of a son, who would attract thousands of female eyes whenever he went bathing on the Tuscan beaches.

"Now Bruno left his frescoes, saying, 'I'm off to the trenches.' He pulled on his raincoat and, as he marched proudly out of the hall, Enzo and the other artists felt their hearts melt. They all adored him, you see.

"It was 1944, did I mention that? . . . Bruno became a much-feared partisan fighter with the battle name Caravaggio, because his enormous artistic gift so much recalled the great artist from Bergamo. Bruno took part in many memorable clashes with the enemy in Monteriggioni. With his cohorts Tartufo [Truffle] and Delfino [Dolphin], he formed a team of feared partisans, capturing German soldiers and handing them over to the Allies. He had no particular political convictions, just his simple belief in freedom; all he wanted was for his country to be liberated from the Nazis.

"It was spring. The plants in the forests were swelling with life, and the first violets had appeared. The sun was warming and the skies clearing; the clouds seemed as if they were chasing one another across the sky, darting into view, then just as suddenly disappearing. It was all pure, all new. And with his artist's eye, Bruno saw it all.

"'The life of a partisan can be hard and full of risks,' he said to his friend Tartufo. 'But you cannot complain in the face of enchantment.' And he stared up at the crystal-clear sky, dazzled.

"Now, Tartufo was not like that. He was a silent and peaceful young man, robust and solid; his head was covered in thick brown curls, and underneath those curls lay a country boy's unfailing common sense. He exchanged a glance with Delfino, then said, 'Bruno, remember that we are at war. The enemy can be very close, even in those bushes yonder. Beauty is fine, but it can hide ugliness.'

"'This is so,' Bruno replied. 'Our foes could be anywhere in these hills, and if they happen across locals bearing weapons, they will shoot them on the spot. Danger is our constant companion. Danger is our muse. Yet we mustn't think about the worst that can happen. We must think about our purpose.' He picked up his machine gun, delicately, as though it were a musical instrument. 'For many years I wielded a brush, and I knew and honored its function, which is to create images—vivid, spiritual, eternal.' He stroked the weapon. 'Now I wield a different tool. And I must in turn honor *its* brutal function, which, in my hands, in this conflict, is to destroy human creatures.'

"Now, Delfino was the youngest of the three patriots, and he was prepared to give his life for the freedom of Italy. He said, 'You are a painter, Bruno. You speak as an intellectual. I'm only a poor farmer from the Chianti hills. You have the gift of the great Caravaggio, you have the spirit of the Renaissance in you.'

"Bruno said, 'Don't say such things. I would be unfit even to tie the great master's shoelaces. Such an artist is a *maestro,* his ability a reflection of God, almost supernatural. I—what am I? . . . I am a part-time painter.' But despite his protest he wore a sly smile that showed he was pleased by the compliment.

"They decided then to have a bite to eat, because at two o'clock they were to meet with the commander, Torricella, to receive new orders.

"Those orders were as follows. The partisans were to continue to fight the Germans, even in small skirmishes if necessary. 'We must try to get hold of their weapons,' Torricella said in an imperious tone. 'Beware, though, because the enemy knows that Chianti is full of our forces, and they will take no prisoners.'

"On June 10 Bruno—together with Tartufo, Delfino, and a new comrade named Lupo [Wolf]—took part in a new assault on an ammunition depot close to Vagliagli.

"'Fire,' called Torricella to signal the attack, and when the partisans rushed toward the Germans, the enemy surrendered almost immediately. These were dramatic days in the struggle; in Rome there was open warfare on the streets, people were dying like flies. Here in Chianti, there was tension among the partisans. So the swiftness of the victory came as a giddy relief.

"But it was not to last. Days later the tranquil air rang again with sounds of gunshots and explosions, and grew rank with the scent of burned gunpowder. Bruno appeared to the men patrolling the banks of the Arbia River and said, 'There is a truck of Germans that has halted close to the cypress forest.'

"'We can approach them from the bottom of the hill where the woods are thicker,' said Delfino, revealing his acute tactical sense.

"They crawled on their hands and knees and soon reached the road, puffing like porcupines. 'There are only four of them,' Bruno whispered; 'let's not kill them but take them prisoner and claim their weapons.' And so they did; then they set fire to the truck and returned down the ravine, where they handed the prisoners over to the commander.

"The oppressive, humid air slowly condensed into great, gray clouds. Tartufo remarked that a storm was inevitable; 'Let's go for shelter in that farmhouse.' Delfino, meanwhile, peered through his binoculars, observing the movements on the road from Vagliagli to Siena. And then the sky split open.

"I tell you, Dario, with the crack of the lightning and the roar of the thunder, together with the unnatural shriek of the truck exploding in the air, it seemed like the inferno had taken over the planet.

"Just then a young peasant girl from the nearby farm cried out for us to come and take shelter. She was beautiful, lithe, her eyebrows black, her eyes vivid blue. The farmer produced some glasses and poured out his very best red. 'You must be partisans,' he said. 'My son is out there, he is one of you. Drink, my young friends, the storm is not over!'

"Hailstones started to fall, clattering on the roof like a team of horses, and the girl was terrified; she picked up an olive branch, then made the sign of the cross and threw some holy water on the ground.

"'You know that hail is ruin for us farmers,' remarked the old peasant.

"'Yes, we know,' replied Delfino. And yet for some odd reason they all burst into laughter.

"Eventually the storm ceased, and Bruno decided it was time to go. As they said good-bye, the farmer turned serious and said, 'Please, don't kill the Germans; they will retaliate on us poor peasants. I fought in the Great War and I know what they are capable of when they're angered.'

"'That's how war is,' Bruno replied in a friendly tone. 'But relax, we shall be prudent.'

"The following day the commander called all the partisans

together and told them that, even though they had very few weapons, more students, laborers, and farmers were joining their cause. 'The Germans will have no mercy, so we must do the same,' he said. 'I have received confirmation that the Allies will drop ammunition and supplies by parachute, because Rome has been liberated and they are heading rapidly toward Siena. Last night, in fact, they dropped some leaflets.' He produced one from the table and read it aloud: 'PATRIOTS! ATTACK THE GERMAN AND FASCIST ENEMY ON ALL FRONTS AND DEFEAT THEM IN THE NAME OF ITALIAN FREEDOM!'

"Now, as you may know, Dario, the River Arbia flows slowly through poplar and alder trees, and the waters break on the rocky beds. Bruno and his companions came across such a natural pool and looked on it with ecstasy. Chub and pike swam in the deep blue water and hid in the cracks. 'Why don't we go for a swim?' Bruno proposed.

"They disrobed in the shade of a massive oak. The sun filtered through the leaves, warming the ice-cold water slightly. Bruno had brought his dog, Partigiana; she was a mixture of several hunting breeds. She keenly watched her master dive into the pool, barking angrily when he plunged deep and escaped her view, then held her head high and alert till he reappeared, water streaming over his muscular frame. He wrung out his hair with his hands, then threw open his arms and exclaimed, 'Oh, how happy I am!'

"The previous day he had been to Siena, where he was briefly reunited with his wife and daughter—did I not mention he was married, Dario?—and his parents, but he was not dispirited by having left them so soon. He was like that—the simple act of swimming in this river was as restorative, for him, as being bathed in family affection. He was always rendered speechless in the face of natural beauty, and today the air was saturated by an aromatic scent of mold and mushrooms, and the ground was covered with dead leaves. He raised his right hand and started gesturing as if he were painting; he brushed the outline of the sweet hills of San Polo and Ama, the small plateau of San Sano, and the forested ditches that marked the steep ravines. 'I have so many paintings to begin once the war is over,' he said, his face and voice overflowing with enthusiasm.

"At this point three armed youngsters approached tentatively. Delfino ran out to meet them, then came back and said, 'They say they are partisans and that they want to join the group, but they are very young and seem scared.'

"'You are welcome,' Bruno called out to them; 'the greater our number, the stronger we are!'

"The oldest of the newcomers reported that the Germans that very morning were in Vagliagli on a truck, stealing olive oil from the farmers. 'The village is being turned inside out and the inhabitants are terrorized.'

"Bruno's mood changed in an instant. 'Let's go,' he said grimly. They left the forest and followed a small trail. The fields were full of wheat as far as the eye could see; irises and poppies gave the image of a blooming garden. It was June 12.

"They reached the main road just outside the village; it was bordered by a low stone wall. From behind a curb they spotted an open truck carrying three soldiers. Bruno, who was crouching behind the wall, suddenly surprised everyone by leaping up and running toward the truck, spraying bullets with his machine gun. Then he was distracted for a split second by the sudden appearance of an oxcart, and stopped shooting lest he hit it. At that moment one of the German's retaliatory bullets tore into his flesh, killing him.

"Delfino and Tartufo fired back, killing one soldier and wounding another. The three young newcomers hid terrified behind the wall.

"The Germans picked up Bruno's body—the corpse of our beloved Caravaggio—threw him onto the back of the truck, and disappeared up the hill in a cloud of dust, leaving a smattering of blood on stone as the only evidence of Bruno's sacrifice. They ended up dumping his body later—in fact, right over there, where I'm pointing.

"There isn't much else to tell. You can imagine the grief for yourself, Dario. Now I've told you what you want to know, so leave me alone, will you?"

We sit in silence for a few moments, but I find I can't quite honor my agreement to let him be. I still have a few questions.

"I'm sorry, Cesarino," I say, "but could you tell me what happened to the others?"

He pauses, as if unwilling to speak, then says, "Tartufo was killed the following month, in the same skirmish in which Delfino took a bullet in the leg."

"So—Delfino survived the war? Is he still alive? Could you tell me his real name?"

He grows impatient and will not meet my eye. "You asked about Caravaggio," he says, "and I've told you about Caravaggio. Don't go asking me for anyone else's story." He rises to his feet. "I've got work to do now, please don't bother me."

He takes my empty glass from me, puts it back into his sack, and heads down the road to his olive grove. I want to call him back—to ask him how he knows so much of Bruno's story: the sights, the sounds, even the scents!—and then I notice for the first time that he walks with a pronounced limp.

"*Grazie*," I call out—for a moment, I think of adding the name *Delfino*, just to see if he will turn back and acknowledge it. Instead, I leave the old man his privacy and return to the monument, where I stand a few moments in silence reflecting on the tragic story I've just heard—the story of an artist, a philosopher, a lover of nature and beauty who inspired ardent and undying love in all who knew him, who was by sheer mischance born into a world that demanded aggression of him and rewarded him with death.

I promise myself to do some research on Bruno Bonci's paintings . . . you might be interested to know that I eventually did and they are quite beautiful. I pick up a wildflower and place it on his monument, and gaze at it in silence with my head hung low.

3:11 P.M.

I spot Don Aldo, the parish priest, entering the cemetery, about 50 yards away. Now in his late seventies, he's definitely one of the more intellectual personalities in the village, yet every time I look at him he strikes me as an achingly lonely old man. Rail thin, he chain-smokes unfiltered Camel cigarettes so incessantly that it's odd now to see him without one; his face is buried in his hands, and his chest is heaving, as though racked with pain. Over the years his smile has become a rarity, and as he roams the streets alone he meets all the *buongiornos* and *buonaseras* from the villagers with the same loving yet sad expression. Despite the low percentage of Tuscans who attend weekly Mass, he manages to fill the church, and its coffers—quite a testament to the attachment the Vagliaglini feel for him.

I've promised myself many times to attend at least one of his services, but I have yet to do so. In truth, I'm spiritually and emotionally removed from church traditions; to me it seems that simply admiring creation in all its open-air magnificence is an entirely suitable way to thank whatever superior entity is responsible. Why, then, submit myself to any constraining religious ritual?

Even so, my respect for Don Aldo is enormous, based on the many theological discussions we've engaged in over a glass of wine at the local bar. Perhaps there were *too* many; we now confine our talks to soccer tactics, but even there we find little agreement, for he is a 4–4–2 formation supporter while I prefer the 4–3–3. He believes in the man-to-man defense, I support the zone. And so it goes . . .

I enter the front of the gate of the cemetery and approach him. But he is immersed in prayer, whispering some verses in Latin, plucking the dried-out flowers from the vases on the tombstones. He keeps a hand on his back while bending down, as if steadying himself. There is something vulnerable and private about him at this moment, so I decide against disturbing him and back away to continue up the road a pace . . .

Oh Lordy

About two years ago I rose one damp morning in early autumn to find that it was raining steadily and fog had filled the valleys. It couldn't have been a worse day to conduct a tour in Chianti. The only ray of light was a metaphorical one: the presence of Cristina. She wore a flowery silk dressing gown and was seated at the breakfast table with her intense, enigmatic smile. *As beautiful as ever,* I thought.

The TV news was on, and the weather forecast was not looking good for the following days. That morning I had to pick up an American couple for a day tour, then drop them off at Florence airport in the evening. It wasn't so much the rain that bothered me as the fog, which reduced visibility to near zero. I was nervous: I knew I had to be in perfect tour-guide form to make up for the terrible weather.

When I got into the van, the windows were all steamed up and I was obliged to turn on the headlights. I started off in the direction of Siena, and although I'd driven that route literally thousands of times, I had to go at a snail's pace or risk missing one of its sharp turns. The journey seemed endless. I tried to cheer myself up by reminding myself that when the sun did come out I would go picking mushrooms with Bartoli and Maura. I imagined the wide variety that thanks to all the moisture would be popping out of the chestnut forests: the cucchi, to eat raw with some olive oil and a drop of lemon; the giallarelle, to mix with a tomato sauce and to serve with steaming homemade tagliatelle; and the precious porcini, to grill on the hearth.

I was so successful in imagining all this that my mouth was watering by the time I parked in front of the hotel. A group of English tourists was filing into a large bus; I eavesdropped on their comments. "So much for sunny Italy," one of them complained; "we might just as well have booked a room in Little Hampton." I felt sorry for them—and for myself as well, because now the temperature had dropped, and I had neglected to wear anything warmer than my usual uniform: a white shirt over a pair of worn jeans and boots.

I was early, so I waited outside beneath a shelter and lit a cigarette. Eventually a woman in her early forties approached me. She wore a red-checked flannel shirt, light blue bell-bottomed jeans, and sneakers; her long hair was unkempt and hung in her eyes. She was plump, with a double chin and small brown eyes. The most riveting thing about her, however, was a large brown mole on her cheek with a very long dark hair protruding from its center.

Without even introducing herself, she said, "I have buried two husbands who smoked. Please refrain from doing so in front of me."

I apologized, a bit shaken by her directness, and flicked the butt in the wet gravel. She was still glaring. I tried to break the ice by telling her I was a bit anxious, as it would be a challenge to give a tour in such foul weather.

"The weather is never bad," she corrected me. "However it is, is the will of the Lord, and you should always praise Him." With that, she cast her eyes skyward, as though the clouds might at that moment dissipate and reveal the Almighty in His splendor, having waited patiently for His cue. "We are blessed by so much generosity," she added.

Then her expression changed and a smile crept over her face, "You must be Dario, our guide for the day." She dropped her leather handbag and to my complete surprise embraced me. "I thank the Lord for having given me the honor of encountering the author of *Too Much Tuscan Sun,*"," she said, giving me a strong squeeze.

Her companion now approached. "Why, honey, don't tell me that this gentleman is Dario!" he said, smiling. He was a tiny figure with a long white beard, decked out in a curious and tight-fitting black suit and a large hat. To my dismay, he joined in the hug from behind me. I found myself encircled by four increasingly constricting arms, while he said, "I thank you, Lord, for such a pleasant encounter. We are blessed by your utter generosity."

Now it was my turn to recite a prayer; I looked up toward the gunmetal-gray sky and thought, *Please, if you do exist, help me out today!*

They boarded the van, and while I loaded their luggage into the trunk, the companion produced a silver container from a pouch and sprayed the interior while murmuring an incomprehensible chant. When I got in the driver's seat and turned on the engine, he asked if I would turn it off for a moment. To my amazement they both grabbed my hands, and this time it was the woman's turn to say, "Oh Lordy, we thank you for your uttermost generosity and plead with you to make this journey memorable and, more important, safe." They fell silent, their eyes shut in meditation, mine wide open as well as my mouth. All I could think was, *Oh boy.*

At last we were able to start. I cleared my throat and said, "Mr. and Mrs. Swanson, right?"—but they corrected me, eerily in unison, "Oh, no, please just call us Starmoon and Late Summer Harvest."

"Ooookay," I replied, deciding to humor them as much as need be. "Well, you said you wanted to visit the abandoned church of San Galgano and then go straight to the airport, is that correct?"

"Yes, Dario, that will be just great," said Late Summer Harvest. I waited for him to thank the Lord again, but he didn't seem to need to this time; so I drove through the gate and headed in direction of the Montagnola area, southwest of Siena.

The weather was still terrible, and more than once I was forced to wipe the windshield with a cloth just to see. To pass the time (and, I admit, to satisfy my curiosity) I asked them which religion they were affiliated with. Starmoon replied that they were followers of the Temple of the Humble Worshippers of the Supreme Entity Who Loves and Protects Us from the Skies. When she finally finished reciting the name, I asked whether all the faith's adherents had such colorful monikers.

"Yes," said Starmoon, "the Master supplies them according to his superior inspiration."

"I see," I replied. "And who is this Master?"

Late Summer Harvest leaned forward and with grave seriousness said, "I am he."

I couldn't think of a suitable response to that—*Good for you* seemed a bit flippant, and *Who appointed you?* perhaps confrontational. So we drove in silence for a while, till I found occasion to start explaining some background to the area's history and culture.

I wasn't long into my spiel when suddenly Starmoon cried, "*Stop!*"

I braked gently, lest my wheels skid on the rain-slick road, and glanced in the rearview mirror while asking what was the matter. Starmoon looked agitated—no, *excited.*

"What's that?" she asked, pointing toward an ancient bridge across the river beside the road. It was barely visible in the fog. I told her it was the bridge of the Pia, erected in the Middle Ages; it led to a castle and was named after the daughter of a local noble family who had been kidnapped and held prisoner for a short time.

Starmoon clapped and said, "It sounds inspiring, don't you think? Why don't we do it there?"

I was sufficiently attuned to this pair's strangeness by now to grow worried about what *it* might be. So I asked—adding, with an unconvincing laugh, "It's nothing *illegal,* I'm sure?"

"Oh, of course not," said Starmoon. "Just a light meditation."

I thought, *Okay, not illegal—just crazy.*

I pulled the van off the road. Since it was still raining thunderously, I offered them the umbrella I had brought with me. Late Summer Harvest politely refused: "No, Dario, we must take what the Lord sends us and be glad of it."

"Come with us!" said Starmoon, grabbing my arm, and I

was taken aback just enough to let her pull me out of the van and up the bridge, where the slippery cobblestones put us at risk of tumbling into the Merse River—there are no railings or barriers on either side. There they knelt and asked me to do the same. We were all of us drenched, yet they raised their eyes heavenward, opened their arms, and said, "Oh Thou Almighty we praise Thee for this day and for having us meet this wonderful person." Then they fell reverently silent. At this point even my underwear was soaked through. I had taken out many strange people in my career as a tour guide, had even written a book about them, but these were beyond doubt the most bizarre.

Minutes later they rose to their feet and said, "Thanks, Dario! We can continue the tour now." They were running with water, their knees covered in mud, but undeterred. On we went.

A few minutes later we reached San Galgano. Abruptly the rain stopped, the clouds parted, a ray of sunshine came through, and a gorgeous rainbow shimmered into being right over the ruined abbey. I couldn't have asked for a more memorable scene.

The abbey was deserted, given the weather—its main attraction is that it no longer has a roof! I parked, and my clients and I ventured outside and stood, alone as far as the eye could see, mesmerized by the beauty. The rainbow formed a perfect arch, its seven beautiful colors positively glowing against the gray sky. I was starting to wonder whether the prayer on the bridge had anything to do with this turnaround.

The abbey had been erected in honor of a legendary local figure named Galgano Guidotti—a soldier who, after a mystical experience in 1180, ran his sword through a nearby rock and swore to live the rest of his life as a religious hermit. He died a year later, only thirty-three years old. His sword is still fixed in the rock, and many believe that the legend of King Arthur's Excalibur has its origins here.

The abbey's first stone was laid in 1185. When the building was finished, it became an active monastery inhabited by Cistercian monks, and for many centuries was under the jurisdiction of Siena. With the fall of the Sienese republic in the sixteenth century, the abbey, too, fell into a slow but inevitable decline. In 1786 the bell tower collapsed and the roof started to cave in, and the possibility was discussed of razing the edifice. Three years later the abbey was completely abandoned, and in relatively recent times the remaining tiles were stolen, leaving the abbey in the near-skeletal condition we find it today.

Adding to the structure's fascination, its four main walls are still sturdy, the naves intact, yet the floor is overgrown with weeds and the windows are obviously empty of glass. A small altar is still in place, and on the hill nearby a little chapel has been built around the rock that contains the saint's stone.

The mist was lifting, leaving the rainbow more vividly visible than before. My guests raced toward the main doorway excitedly, while I stayed a few steps behind. They entered the ancient church jumping up and down like kids entering Disneyland. Once inside they looked at each other and said, "Yes, yes! Let's do it here." I thought, *Here we go again.*

They knelt before the altar, motioning me to do likewise. Starmoon passed me a small book covered in smooth black leather. She then took a white mantle from her back and placed it over my shoulders. "Dario, turn to page seventy-seven and please read the first paragraph for us. Oh, and if possible," she added, "it would be great if you could keep a solemn tone and raise your palm toward the sky."

I nodded my agreement—what choice did I have?—and

read aloud in the roofless deserted church: "I have been designated by your worshippers to receive the gift of being able to marry before you these two humble souls. They will promise to serve you faithfully for the rest of their days . . ." I paused for a second as I realized that I was actually conducting a wedding ceremony. They were still kneeling beside me with their heads bowed, and because I could think of no reason *not* to continue, I cleared my throat and read on. "These your son and daughter are now united in eternity to serve you and divulge your scriptures. Now to end the ceremony and to prove your legacy they exchange their blood . . ." From the corner of my eye I could see Late Summer Harvest producing a small penknife from his pocket, and I lurched to a halt. Starmoon stretched out her arm; he cut gently into her wrist just deeply enough to bring forth a single drop of blood, then performed the same operation on himself. They pressed their wrists together and spent a few moments intensely meditating, eyes clamped shut. I realized that not only had I stopped reading, I had started staring, and my jaw was hanging open.

A few moments later they stood up, smiling, and Late Summer Harvest said to me, "Now to conclude the ceremony, place your hands on our heads and say *Let us rejoice before the Almighty.*" I obeyed, after which they both embraced me, and Late Summer Harvest told me, "To thank you, I give the name Rainbow Over the Abbey."

I managed to murmur some words of apparently sincere-sounding thanks; then we all sat down and from their rucksack they produced a bottle of grappa. "Let us drink and rejoice," said Late Summer Harvest—welcome enough words to me. They passed me the bottle, I took a small swig and passed it back, and to my astonishment they chugged down the entire contents in just a few gulps. Starmoon choked for a second, then looked at me with an unembarrassed smile. She took off her necklace, placed it around my neck, and said, "Now, Rainbow Over the Abbey, we *have* to go see the sword in the stone!"

On the short walk the newlyweds kissed and held hands tightly. When we reached the door of the tiny, round chapel, we entered in silence, and I gestured to where the sword and stone lay protected beneath a glass enclosure. They seemed disappointed; in fact Late Summer Harvest scowled, rubbed his beard, then removed his hat and scratched his head, and eventually said, "It is the will of the Lord that we cannot touch the sword." They both placed their hands on the glass cover, clearly leaving their fingerprints, then turned to me and said, "Okay, we're ready to go to Florence."

As if prompted by this change in mood, it started raining heavily again. When we got back into the van I asked if they wanted to have a bite to eat; they replied that they ate only fruits that had fallen naturally from the trees, and had taken for this trip some special pills that provided them with all the nourishment they required.

On the drive to the airport Starmoon, probably due to the effects of the grappa, fell sound asleep, with her hand twirling the hair from her mole. Late Summer Harvest remained silent, still sulking, it seemed, about not being able to touch the ancient sword of San Galgano.

When we reached the main road and were getting close to the airport, he pointed out a villa perched on the hill and asked me about it. Worried that he had received some new inspiration from above, I explained that it was a Renaissance structure belonging to a private family. He rubbed his beard thoughtfully and said, "Gosh, I wonder why they built it so close to the highway?" I couldn't tell if he was serious or not, so I simply replied, "It's a shame, isn't it?"

I parked in front of the terminal and unloaded the luggage, and again they both embraced me and thanked their supreme entity for such a wonderful day. "Good-bye, Rainbow Over the Abbey," they said as we parted; "we hope to meet you again soon in some other life. The end of the world is nigh."

"How nigh?" I asked, alarmed after so much talk of love and gratitude during the day.

"Judging by the scriptures," Starmoon replied gravely, "a couple of weeks."

I left them at the airport, still in their wet, muddy clothes, imagining them sprinkling the plane with their holy water and chanting more prayers airborne.

I was ravenous by now, so on the way home I decided to look for a nearby trattoria. I still couldn't get over how outlandish my last clients had been. I had met many weird people but these two definitely took the cake! I wondered whether, at the beginning of my career, I would have been able to handle such a situation so smoothly. I had even conducted a wedding!

I took the first exit and drove through a small town, where I spotted what seemed to be a suitable restaurant—with a curious name: Pedal & Fork. I parked in front, and saw displayed in the window some huge *fiorentina* steaks and freshly made *pici* noodles. *Looks good,* I thought.

When I entered the restaurant a couple was being turned away by a very large, goateed man in a chef's hat with the words, "Sorry, we're fully booked." The dining room was deserted, but each table had a RESERVED sign placed in the center. I shrugged and was about to leave myself when the chef came my way, avidly puffing a Tuscan cigar. He was wearing a white collarless shirt, checked black-and-white pants, and a pair of white clogs. He stopped to deposit his cigar ash in a glass ashtray with a Cinzano logo, and since he was right there I decided to try my luck. "Any chance of getting something to eat?" I asked.

"If you're hungry, sure," he replied in a low voice. He plucked one of the RESERVED signs from a table. "Take a seat."

When I complied, he didn't hand me a menu but simply said, "Today we have *ribollita* or *pici alla puttanesca*, and steak or mixed roast." I decided on the *pici* as my first course with steak for the main, then asked about wines. "No wine list," he replied; "you have a choice of red or white *della casa,* and I would suggest that you don't order water as it makes you rusty and the fish pee in it." I settled for the red and decided to take his advice regarding the water, considering that I had really seen enough of the stuff during the day—and it was *still* coming down.

While I waited for my food I couldn't help thinking back to my last clients. I took off the necklace Starmoon had given me and took a look: It was a small medallion with a moon surrounded by stars, tied to a simple silver chain. Rather pretty, but I decided not to wear it so I wrapped it in a paper napkin and put it in my inner pocket.

At that moment a hefty woman came out of the kitchen followed by two teenagers, one a tall, skinny girl with a winning smile, the other a boy some years younger—I guessed him to be fifteen—with a ponytail and a cheeky grin on his freckled face. The chef sat down with the kids, and the woman returned to the kitchen.

I was rather perplexed when another group entered the

restaurant and asked for a table, and were sent away with apologies because the restaurant was booked. Why, I wondered, hadn't I been sent packing? . . . I decided to ask at the end of the meal. In the meantime I settled in and was enjoying the ambience; it was a cozy place, and the walls were covered with photos of legendary Italian cyclists past and present. I recognized the two all-time greats, Gino Bartali and Fausto Coppi, the cyclists who had dominated the scene pre- and postwar, and was impressed that they were all autographed and dedicated to one Giovanni.

Minutes later the woman came back out of the kitchen and served both her family and me the first course. While I was devouring my *pici*, the large chef, whom I guessed to be Giovanni, slapped his son on the back of his head and said, "Will you stop cleaning that shit from your nails with your fork when you're at the table?" His wife joined in by exclaiming, "While we're on the subject, who wiped their ass with my socks last night, eh?" The daughter ended the disquisition by saying, "Don't look at me, I'm constipated, it's been three days since I went to the toilet."

I was so startled I dropped my fork on the plate. What was going on today? Had the entire world gone crazy, or was I dreaming?

I stared at my plate for what seemed a small eternity, then Giovanni stood up and laughed uproariously, as did all his family. He then added a chair to the table and invited me to join them for the second course.

I thought it would be impolite to turn them down, so I went over and sat next to the mother. They turned out to be wonderful company. They explained, still giggling, that when they were in the kitchen they had purposely decided to make up that little scene to see what my reaction would be; they were simply having fun.

With the ice broken, I asked why all the tables were reserved but nobody had turned up yet. Giovanni, again puffing away on his cigar, said it was his habit; if someone entered the restaurant and didn't inspire him, he would simply point out the reserved tables and send them away.

Then he took out a grappa of his own production, and as we drank he explained the autographed photos on the wall. In the 1950s he had been a professional cyclist, racing in a few Giri d'Italia and Tours de France. I was fascinated, being an avid *ciclista* myself. He regaled me with stories of those heroic days when athletes raced up the Alps with heavy, old-fashioned bicycles, on dirt roads so steep even motorbikes had difficulty following. He was simply a *domestique*, never in the spotlight; it was tough, he explained, and the wages were ridiculously low compared with the inhuman fatigue they had to face every day.

He then started pouring out a liqueur he and his wife had made out of walnuts. She had a friendly face but didn't talk much, instead listening to her husband's stories while gazing at him in admiration. He told me that even today, some of the old champs came to visit him in the trattoria.

Suddenly our conversation was interrupted by the arrival of a large group. Giovanni got up to greet them, and I watched as he turned some away with a shrug and a "Sorry, booked up," while inviting the ones he knew or whose looks he liked to sit down.

As I paid my bill I promised to return, and Giovanni realized that he hadn't even asked my name. For a moment I thought of saying, *Rainbow Over the Abbey—Rain to my friends*, but the impulse passed.

As I drove home through the seemingly endless downpour,

I hoped I would find Cristina before the fireplace, and indeed I did. I gave her the full lowdown on my incredible day; she covered her mouth as she laughed, then commented that she couldn't believe how many bizarre people I attracted, advising me not to bother including any of this in my book; no one would believe it.

We opened a bottle of red and roasted some chestnuts on the glowing embers, then just gazed at the flames until she fell asleep, her head on my lap. I gently caressed her hair while watching her dream in the flickering firelight.

3:58 P.M.

It appears that Don Aldo has left the cemetery—his little Fiat 500 is no longer parked in front of the entrance—so I decide to go back in. The wrought-iron gate creaks as I push it open, making the quiet that follows more profound. I always like the peaceful atmosphere of cemeteries, or, as we call them in Italy, the *campi santi* (sacred fields)—a term more poetic, less dramatic, as is so often the case in Italian.

I hear the snorting of a horse and some distant voices echoing down in the valley. The light is still brilliant and reflects off the marble tombstones, most of which are polished and well tended by the deceased's relatives. Almost all the vases are filled with fresh flowers, and I notice that during my absence a couple of new graves were added. I recognize both names engraved on them, and I look at the small photos: one of an old woman who until last year had been active in the village community, the other of a man we called Radar, due both to his Dumbo-sized ears and to his uncanny ability to forecast the weather. I remember him on a clear, cloudless day looking up at the sky and confidently predicting pouring rain within an hour; sure enough, it was soon coming down cats and dogs.

I walk through the section dedicated to the children. It's heartbreaking to see the evidence of so much infant mortality, common here until the 1940s.

On my way out my eyes fall on the tomb of Tonio, an old man of whom I was particularly fond and with whom I had shared a splendid experience that I described in the final chapter of my previous book. I smile, looking at his photo and recalling all the stories he had told me—usually involving the intimate details of his sex life when he was in his nineties and, by his own estimation, an unstoppable love machine. But there were other stories, too, and one in particular that I will always remember . . .

Tonio's Last Story

The last time I met Tonio he was polishing a shrine dedicated to the Madonna in a small cave that he and some other members of the community had dug from volcanic rock. He pedaled there daily to tend the sacred spot with loving care, leaving his bicycle propped against the wall. Knowing he would be pleased to see me, I called out, "Tonio, how are you?"

"Very well, *nini*," he replied, using an affectionate expression the elderly employ when speaking to someone younger. He came outside and placed his cap on his head, then sat on the bench overlooking the valley and invited me to do the same. His eyes were a bit duller than usual—they seemed to have lost their characteristic spark—and he looked wan and pale. Strangely, he didn't give me his usual full recounting of what he and his wife had been up to the previous night. He remained still, gazing at the lush Chianti valleys, until, to bring him out of this funk, I asked whether he was willing to improvise one of his stories for me. To my relief, he nodded.

Tonio's creative capacity was amazing; he was a skilled carpenter, a *maestro* in forging wrought iron, and a very fine landscape painter; his wine would have left Bacchus impressed, his grappa was the smoothest I'd tasted, his olive oil divine—and to top it all off he was a dazzling storyteller. All I had to do was to give him a subject, and he would immediately spin it into an unforgettable yarn.

At that moment a van from a village bakery drove by, and inspired by the warm, fresh aroma that lingered in its wake, I said to the old man, "How about a story about bread?" Tonio raised his cap, scratched his head, and a few moments later began narrating in his soft, lyrical singsong voice.

"Listen, *nini,*" he said, "there was a widow who had a daughter. They were very poor, and to makes things even harder on them she was very sick. So everything was in the hands of the little girl. She had to look after her mother and also had to work—they had no other means. Every day she would go to the forest close by the village and make two bundles of wood. One she would use to light the home fire and cook; the other she would sell. Since she was small and weak, she only had strength enough to cut down the youngest shoots and saplings, but even so she managed to get by.

"The forest, alas, belonged to a rich baron, and one day while riding through the woods he saw that someone was cutting down his younger trees. Hoping to catch the thief, and he started coming to the forest every day. And so it was that one day he spotted the young girl cutting some young branches. 'So it is you who dares to cut down my trees?' he said.

"'Yes, it is I,' the girl replied in a mortified voice.

"'Why do you come here? The forest isn't yours and you are ruining all my young shoots!'

"'I know, and I am sorry. I try to do my best, and maybe I do ruin your trees. But I am alone, my mother is very sick, and we have nothing. I come here because it is close to our shack, and so I can make a couple of bundles a day. I always try to make two, one to sell at the market and the other to burn in the fireplace to keep us warm.'

"'I understand,' said the baron, touched by pity. 'Well . . . tomorrow you may return; but let it be the last time.'"

Tonio paused a moment; so far he had yet to mention the word *bread,* and my anticipation grew pleasantly.

"So, *nini,*" he continued, "the following day the young girl returned to the forest. When she had finished collecting her usual bundle of twigs, the baron again arrived and gave her a large loaf of bread. 'Take it and eat it with your mother, and don't ever return to my forest.'

"The girl went home. She wanted to eat the loaf, but she thought it was too much for her, so instead she gave it to the doctor who came daily to visit her sick mother, and whom she had as yet not been able to pay.

"The doctor thanked her and that evening at dinner told his maid to slice open the beautiful loaf. As soon as the knife pierced the first crusty layer they found that it was full of gold coins.

"'Well fancy that,' the doctor said to his maid, 'those two acting so poor, and then they fill up their bread with gold coins! Seeing that they have never paid me for any of my visits I shall definitely keep the money!'

"In the meantime the poor girl went to seek for wood in a more distant forest, but the walk was too far and despite all her efforts she never managed to gather more than a single bundle. So eventually she decided to return to the baron's forest, but also to take great care that he wouldn't see her. This worked well for a few days, until inevitably one morning she met the baron again. 'What are you doing here?' he asked angrily. 'Did you not promise me you would never return? Did I not give you the bread?'

"'Yes, I did promise, and you did give me the bread.'

"'Then why are you here? You cannot so quickly have used up the bread.'

"The girl explained that she had not used the bread at all; she had given the loaf to the doctor because of all the times he had come to visit her mother without receiving any payment.

"'You should not have done that,' the baron said. 'Even so, I will allow you once again to return tomorrow, but believe me this must be the very last time.'

"The following day, while she was cutting the wood, the baron arrived with another very large loaf of bread and gave it to the girl, instructing her to share it with her mother. In the evening she sat down and stared at the bread, contemplating whether to eat it or not. She finally decided to give it to the local priest who came daily to assist her mother, mixing her medicines and comforting her spiritually; it was the least she could do to thank him.

"That evening the priest sliced open the loaf and found the same surprise, and thought, *Imagine those two pretending to be poor, and now they send me all these gold coins. Perhaps they were too ashamed to give them to me outright and so baked them in the bread. Well, I will not embarrass them, then, by mentioning it.* So the priest kept the money and never thanked the girl.

"Again the girl went to the far-off forest and again she tried her hardest, but the long walk left her with strength enough only for one bundle for her home fire, and none left to sell. So again she broke her promise and returned to the baron's forest.

"After a few weeks the baron went for a walk and was surprised to see the girl again in his woods. 'What did you do with the bread I gave you?' he asked.

"The girl replied, 'You must forgive me but I was so much in debt to the priest that I gave it to him.' Again the baron allowed her to return one final time the following day, and again he gave a large loaf of bread and made her vow that this time she and her mother would eat it. Before he left her, he also said that if he found her again in his woods he would call his guards and have her arrested.

"Once she was back home, she decided to eat the bread immediately before she could think of someone else who might be more deserving of it. But as she sliced into the loaf her knife met something hard that she couldn't cut. She plunged her fingers in the soft interior and pulled out a solid gold crucifix. It bore writing on its reverse side, but the girl had never been to school and couldn't read it.

"The following morning she returned to the woods, this time hoping to find the baron and to give him back the crucifix that had, she thought, accidentally fallen into the dough. The baron did return, and when he saw the girl he grew very angry and shouted, 'Despite all I've done for you, you again return to steal from my forest!'

"'No indeed, Baron,' the girl replied, 'this time I have not come to make any bundles, as you can see I have no strings with me to tie them. Today I come only to give you back the crucifix that accidentally fell into the dough.'

"The baron couldn't understand, for he had placed 200 gold

coins inside the loaf, not a crucifix. Mystified, he took it from her. Seeing the writing on the back, he read it. It said:

"IF I HAD WANTED HER TO BE RICH, I WOULD HAVE MADE HER SO.

"The baron realized that he had been part of a divine event, a true miracle. With tears in his eyes, he embraced the girl and said, 'I will keep the crucifix, and in return I give to you the entire forest. Come when you like, cut all the wood you need, it is yours!'

"And so every day the girl would go and collect her two bundles, one to sell in the market and the other to light the fire and heat up the soup for her sick mother. That's it, *nini.*"

As usual, I thanked Tonio with a handshake, once again dazzled by his capacity to improvise stories as rich and resonant as any fables or folktales. He made the sign of the cross before the Madonna. I accompanied him back to his bicycle, where he said, *"Addio, nini."*

"See you tomorrow, Tonio," I said with a wave.

"Se Dio vuole"—if God wishes—my ninety-year-old friend replied.

I never saw him again. That night Tonio decided it was time to go. His son told me at the funeral that he was found in the morning with a smile on his face.

4:47 P.M.

I find myself walking on the ridge of the hill where it is said my village originated. Farther up the road, in a cypress forest, four Etruscan tombs were recently unearthed dating from around 500 B.C. They are very large and likely belonged to a noble family who, according to the archaeologists, came here on vacation to enjoy the sweet climate and beautiful scenery—exactly the reasons so many tourists visit even today.

I take a narrow path that leads to a small group of stone houses attached to one another, forming a *borgo* named Cignano. The silence here is eerily unreal. It is, in part, the silence of eternity. Documents from as early as A.D. 998 mention this location.

I spot a tall live oak tree with a massive trunk, and placing my hands on its bark I accidentally uncover an ants' nest. On a whim I haul myself up to the lower branch, then decide to climb all the way to the top.

From up here I can see my old house close to the tiny hamlet in San Leonino down in the valley, on the west, and facing east the splendid presbytery of San Leonardo. Nobody is in sight; Cignano appears abandoned.

I remain in contemplation for a while, perched on the highest branch of the tree. I, too, feel eternity ebb around me as I face my old house, which represents the past, stirring more memories . . .

San Leonino Days

At the age of twenty, I decided to go and live on my own, and I was lucky enough to find available a portion of an ancient farmhouse in San Leonino owned by a friend of mine. The structure—divided into two apartments—was perched on a beautiful hill; thanks to this advantageous position I could enjoy spectacular views through windows facing both east and west. In the bathroom I could shave to the sight of dawn over the hills, and in the evening sit on the windowsill with a glass of wine, taking in full majesty of the sun slowly setting behind Montemaggio.

My friend Carlo let me have the apartment for a nominal rent, but warned me that there was no heating—the sole fireplace in the house was located in the other half—and that the winter would likely be long and miserable. The second apartment had been rented to a very unfriendly Croatian lady—who because of her pronounced lower lip and her vicious character I nicknamed "Jaws"—so it seemed the fireplace was destined to remain off limits to me.

When winter arrived I realized the full import of Carlo's warning. Nights were of course the coldest. In bed I was forced to wear a thick wool ski cap that I pulled down over my face, and one night I reached for the glass of water I kept on my bedside table only to find it hardened into ice.

Another time my refrigerator stopped functioning. The repairman I summoned explained patiently that the appliance was fine; it wasn't working simply because the room temperature was lower than the thermostat setting. When I invited friends over to dinner, they teased me by saying that mine was the only house where instead of taking off your coat upon entering, you were obliged to don an extra one! The only means of getting warm was to drink red wine, and God only knows how many liters I drained during those long winters.

To make things even tougher, in those years I was the proud owner of a motorbike. Because I couldn't afford both a car and the machine that had become for me a passion, I decided to keep the latter. I had a job working in a very large winery, and to keep warm on my early-morning winter drives, I would set the alarm half an hour earlier than usual to get dressed. I wore three pairs of socks and a pair of long johns (my great-uncle's) beneath a pair of jeans, over which I donned a pair of Gore-Tex trousers, which I tucked into a pair of leather boots, which I covered in turn with a pair of overboots. Over my torso I pulled a long-sleeved Lycra T-shirt, three wool sweaters, and a Gore-Tex jacket. I donned undergloves, gloves, and overgloves; a thick scarf, an underhelmet, a crash helmet, and an overhelmet. I also had a heating device to warm the handlebars. Despite all this I suffered like a beast over the endless 15-mile drive. When I arrived at work, my companions would take great joy in pointing out my resemblance to the Michelin Man.

One Sunday morning, while I was busy cleaning my motorbike, I heard the phone ring in the living room. It was Paolo, a close friend of mine who had the annoying habit of shouting into the receiver. "Lower your voice, Paolo," I said after he bellowed his greeting. "I'm only a few miles away, not in Australia!"

"Be a sport, Dario, will you?" he said in a voice only slightly less booming. "I've got a very important exam at the university next week, and my brother Marcello is driving me nuts. He keeps quarreling with Dad—you know what it's like, he's only eighteen, difficult age—anyhow there's so much tension in the house I can't study!"

"Paolo, you know my house is always open to you. If you want to come spend a few days, you're more than welcome."

"No, no, Dario, you must be joking, I don't want to freeze to death. I was thinking of sending Marcello over." Before I could sputter out an objection, he said, "Thanks, Dario, I knew I could count on you!"

"But—I've never met him," I blurted before he could hang up.

"Oh, you'll like him, he's a good guy."

"You just said he's difficult! Honestly, Paolo, I don't know about this."

"Dario, I promise you, he'll cause you no trouble. And I really need this."

"Well," I muttered, giving in, "if it's really necessary for you and you assure me he won't be a problem, I'll do it in the name of our friendship." He thanked me a few times more, then swiftly rang off before I could add anything else.

That same evening Marcello arrived. From the bathroom window, I watched him park his black Fiat in front of the farmhouse. He took a black suitcase from the backseat and set it on the ground.

"Need a hand?" I called out the open window.

He looked up, shrugged, said, "I'm okay," then opened the trunk and produced a guitar case and then a black amplifier. And I started to worry.

I ran downstairs and flung open the front door to admit him. He was quite a handsome young man, all in black—elegant black jacket over black turtleneck sweater, black pressed trousers, and very impressive black army boots. A closer glance revealed that his car was covered with stickers for the then popular band the Cure, which helped explain his fashion sense—so close to that of the group's lead singer, Robert Smith.

He removed his right black glove and gave me a high five. "Welcome, Marcello," I said, swallowing a gulp of dread. I picked up his suitcase and led him up the stairs. To break the ice I asked if the guitar was his hobby.

"Um, *no,*" he replied in voice sharp with annoyance. "The *bass* guitar. That's why I need the amplifier."

"Ah," I said, feeling somehow rebuked.

I showed him his room and told him to make himself feel at home while I popped down to the village store to get a few things for dinner. He watched me go with a curious smirk.

Returning from my errand I was shocked to hear music blaring from the direction of my house, which was still at least a mile away. My first thought was of Jaws, who would certainly raise a fuss over the noise; I could easily imagine her lecturing me on my doorstep, wagging her finger threateningly before my nose. Fortunately, when I got closer I saw that her car was gone, and sighed in relief.

I rushed up the steps two at a time and passed the threshold. The noise was deafening, the windows rattling in their frames. I threw open the door and found Marcello wearing only his black underwear, performing a kind of pogo dance while the stereo blasted a song I now recognized as "The Sisters of Mercy." With my hands over my ears I dashed over to the console and cranked down the volume.

Marcello abruptly stopped dancing, then again turned on me his maddening sneer and said, "Just like Dad."

We stood in tense silence for a few moments until suddenly his expression changed, and in a jovial tone he said that while I was out he'd made a few changes to his room—because, he explained, "It had a negative energy."

I followed him down the corridor to the guest room. Marcello proudly showed me how he had rearranged the cupboard with the bed and the writing table, which was certainly no problem. But he had also nailed to the walls a number of macabre Gothic crosses, and had made the bed with a hideous black coverlet with a golden cross sewn in the center. I tried to force a smile. "Very nice, Marcello," I said, trying not to imagine the amount of time it would take to fill those holes in the wall with putty once he'd gone. "Nice bedspread," I added, gilding the blatant lie with an appreciative stroking of its smooth, velvety nap.

"Glad you like it," he said, beaming. "I got it cheap at a flea market. The vendor told me it was used by priests to cover the coffins during actual funerals!" I withdrew my hand in a heartbeat.

"Original, yes. Very . . . original." It was the first and only adjective I could manage. "Well . . . I guess I'll go and take a shower, then prepare dinner." I made my way out of the refurbished bedroom, trying not to touch anything with the hand that had been contaminated by the impious cloth.

When I got out of the bathroom, I was overcome by a thick fog and a sweet aroma. Marcello had exchanged the regular lightbulbs for some of an impractically dim blue hue, and had also lit some terrible incense sticks all around the house. Meanwhile he was busy smoking grass from an enormous pipe while comfortably leafing through a book he'd plucked from a pile he'd stacked next to the couch. I was horrified when I noticed he'd covered all of his volumes with the funeral announcements used regularly in Italy to inform locals about recent deaths; he must have peeled them right off the walls for his own macabre use.

"What are you reading, Marcello?" I asked, trying to behave as though I hadn't noticed anything strange. He raised his head slowly, his eyes stoned red, and drawled, "*The Dawn of the Living Dead.* Want a drag, Dario?" He reached out to pass me the pipe.

"No, thanks," I replied, my eye drawn to the name of the departed on the book cover. FRANCO LOMBARDI, AGED 79. As it happened, I knew him; he'd owned a flower shop. I hadn't, however, known he'd died. And this was not the way I would have chosen to find out.

My brief reminiscence of the late Signore Lombardi was interrupted by the trill of the telephone in my bedroom. I rushed to pick up the receiver; it was Paolo. I closed the door.

"So, how's my little brother doing? You two getting along, becoming buddies?"

"Well," I said, "apart from the fact that he's blasted his terrible music, rearranged the furniture, changed all the lightbulbs, and dresses like a Gothic bum, he's fine." I hadn't meant to deliver such an outburst, but I couldn't help myself; nor could I stop now. "I don't know what to expect next—maybe Nosferatu showing up for dinner? Wouldn't surprise me."

"What's wrong with him?" Paolo asked, as though he'd heard nothing I said.

"What's *wrong* with him?" I blurted. "He's only been here a few hours and my house looks like a coven of satanists has moved in. Come and fetch him immediately, or I'll see to it that the next book he covers has *your* funeral announcement on it."

Paolo laughed, then in an appeasing tone said, "Come on, Dario, why not look at the funny side of it? And it is only for a few days. You're a real sport, I mean it; and I appreciate you doing this in the name of our friendship."

Speechless, I put down the receiver and returned to the living room where Marcello was still reading and puffing on his pipe. When he saw me glaring at him, he stood up, unfazed, and said he was too hungry to wait for dinner, he was going to grab a quick sandwich in the closest village, and I could join him if I liked.

"Yes, let's get out of here," I replied, thinking it a good idea to get away from the house for a while.

I got into his black Fiat, and he climbed into the driver's seat. He pulled on a pair of black leather gloves, cracked his knuckles, and put the car in first gear—then second—then third, and finally fourth. I clenched my hand on the grip as we darted off at full speed. The village was only 5 miles away, so I said a prayer and kept my mouth shut, thinking my life would only be in peril for only a few minutes; but to my amazement Marcello tore right past the small village, then whipped the steering wheel around for a spectacularly daring 180-degree turn and roared onto SS 222.

"You passed Castellina," I pointed out.

"Yep," he replied nonchalantly. "First I've got a little business to do in Florence, shouldn't take a minute."

"But Florence is an hour away!" I protested.

"Nah," he said, his sneer creeping back onto his face. "Twenty minutes, tops. Trust me."

I must admit that despite my stomach's continual flip-flops, and my fear that at any moment we would plunge off a cliff, Marcello was a great pilot. He kept his eyes glued to the road and his hands on the steering wheel as he guided the Fiat over the twisting, deserted roads that led to Florence at heart-stopping speed.

He inserted a cassette of some music unknown to me, and with his head bouncing up and down he followed the rhythm, oblivious to my requests that he slow the hell down.

In no time we reached the city. He headed toward Porta Romana, then Piazzale Michelangelo, and finally slammed his foot on the brakes near a small marble fountain, bringing us to a sudden, lurching stop.

He rolled down his window, pursed his lips, and emitted a piercing whistle. A short furtive-looking man suddenly jumped out of the bushes and without a word approached our car. He put his head inside the open window and handed Marcello a small envelope, which Marcello exchanged for a roll of a few hundred thousand-lire notes. The man counted quickly, then tucked them into his inner jacket pocket and disappeared silently from whence he'd come.

Clearly, I had just met Marcello's dope supplier.

Marcello handed me the keys and asked if I was willing to drive. Given the alternative, I certainly was. We swapped seats, and as I turned the car toward Poggio Imperiale and then onto Via Senese, I had the impression that we were being followed—I could see a car in the rearview mirror that was keeping suspiciously close to us. Even when I passed Bottai and entered the freeway, it remained behind us, declining to pass us even when I purposely slowed down. My worry increased as it dutifully followed when I took the San Donato exit. For his part, Marcello was too busy rolling his second joint to share my fear.

I was close to panic when, fortunately, the mysterious car took a side road before we reached Castellina in Chianti, and disappeared.

We walked to the village to get something to eat, but to my dismay the only place open was the local Communist bar where inside a group of old men were busy playing cards, and everyone else, as usual, was discussing how great it would be to live in the Soviet Union.

I ordered a ham sandwich. Marcello, with the insatiability of the stoned, wolfed down six cream buns and quaffed a couple of beers. While I waited for him to finish, I noticed that the walls were covered with framed photos of Lenin and some late Italian Communist party leader. I couldn't suppress a giggle when I noticed that even the bartender had a mustache that resembled Stalin's.

Eventually we left the patrons to continue their heated discussion on whether the quality of life was better in Bulgaria or Poland, and headed back toward the car. During the short drive home, I thought about how ridiculous those people were—probably none of them had ever traveled beyond Siena. How I would have enjoyed taking them over the Iron Curtain, showing them firsthand what they defined as "paradise," and then dumping them there.

These nasty thoughts didn't last long—it was now 1:00 A.M., and I was exhausted. As soon as I lay my ski-capped head on my pillow, I fell sound asleep.

Two hours later I was suddenly wakened by a wave of deafening noise. It didn't take me long to realize that Marcello was practicing scales on his bass guitar, with the amplifier on. I shouted for him to stop but the terrible *dum dum dum* continued. I got up and marched angrily into the living room, where Marcello was standing on my couch as if on a stage, decked out in black and wearing sunglasses. Before I could say anything the doorbell started ringing insistently. Feeling like I might go crazy,

I ordered Marcello to stop immediately, then opened the door. It was, of course, Jaws, looking quite a sight in an absurdly flowery pink dressing gown, with large plastic hair curlers. Before I could either explain or apologize, she emptied a glass of ice-cold water in my face and spewed out a series of what must have been Croatian curse words, which I am fortunately unable to translate. She then returned to her side of the house, slamming the door behind her.

Marcello, who had observed the entire scene, now laughed like a maniac. "Cute neighbor you have there, Dario," he said. "Congratulations." Seeing the unamused look on my wet, cold face, he adopted a more serious expression and promised solemnly not to make any more noise.

Even so, I felt that the situation was out of control . . . and getting worse by the minute. I went back to bed and tossed and turned in frustration till sheer exhaustion pulled me back to sleep.

The following morning I was surprised to see that Marcello wasn't home. I found a brief note pinned to the door that offered his apologies for all the previous day's events and said that he had gone shopping to look for a new broom because, as he put it, "Yours no longer works."

As I went through the lengthy process of donning all my various layers of clothes for the ride to work, I thought that maybe Marcello wasn't such a bad guy after all.

The morning was, of course, absolutely frigid. Everything was white, even the sky; the tiny creek was frozen, the trees naked except for a few evergreens, and the fields covered with frost. When I passed over them on my motorbike, I could hear the frozen blades of grass crackling beneath the tires. Everything was eerily still; most of the wildlife was either still asleep or in hibernation. It was a lonely, yet exhilarating feeling.

At the end of my shift I returned home, fearing that I'd walk in on the middle of some improvised rave. Instead I was both pleased and impressed to find Marcello sweeping up the house with a brand-new black broom that he proudly showed me. He then opened the refrigerator and pointed out all kinds of expensive goodies he had filled it with.

"No hard feelings, Dario?" he said.

I shrugged. "No hard feelings."

He grinned, then brought out a sack, from which he produced a collection of priest's robes and a small shrine. He proudly explained that he had found them in the small abandoned church of San Leonardo.

Before I could offer any kind of opinion the doorbell rang again. Wary of another attack by Jaws, I opened the door cautiously. There on the threshold were two men in trench coats. The taller waved a badge before my face and said in a firm voice, "You're under arrest." Before I could object or even think he grabbed my arm, dragged me downstairs, and pushed me into a car that I recognized as the one that had followed us the previous night.

I started to protest, but they told to keep my mouth shut and to save my explanations for the *commissario.* As the car peeled away I noticed Jaws in her window, observing the scene with a satisfied grin.

During the entire drive the detective next to me glared at me in disgust. When we arrived at the station, he accompanied me down a long, drab corridor, then locked me in a room with iron bars on the windows. As soon as he left me on my own, I felt an urge to burst into tears—partly in despair, partly in rage. I didn't even want to think what kind of trouble Marcello had landed me in, but I hoped for both our sakes I never saw him again, because I would strangle him with my bare hands.

Half an hour later I was taken from the holding cell to an office where, to my horror, I saw Marcello comfortably seated before an officer's hardwood desk. The officer ordered me to take a seat as well; then the owner of a mini market came in and pointed his finger at Marcello. "That's him all right," he said. "*He's* the one I saw stealing this morning, taking the broom and shoving it down his coat. And I'm sure it wasn't the only thing he took, judging by the awkward way he waddled out to the parking lot!"

The fool had actually shoplifted. I tried to imagine him thinking he could hide all that food *and* a broom underneath his long black coat, and get away with it. *Idiot.*

My thoughts jarred back to the present as the door opened again, and an imposing middle-aged man in thick glasses whom I guessed to be the *commissario* entered.

He crossed the room with his eyes glued to a paper he was reading attentively, then sat down in the chair on the opposite side of the desk, beneath the huge portrait of the Italian president Pertini. He then placed the document on the desk, raised his head, and gave a start when he saw Marcello; he stared at the boy for several moments, apparently shocked.

Marcello, his cheeky smirk stamped on his face, broke the silence by saying, "Hello, Dad."

In the end, I was released. Marcello's father was very understanding; he apologized for all the trouble I'd been through and ordered an officer to drive me back home.

But that house would not be my home much longer. At the age of twenty-three I started to suffer from rheumatism and asthma, and was forced to leave before another brutal winter set in.

Paolo did not pass his exam. Twenty years later, he works as a waiter in a restaurant. Each time we meet he recalls the time he sent his renegade brother to me, and we laughingly relive the whole calamity over a glass of red wine.

Marcello has changed his life almost completely. True, he still wears only black . . . but this is because he is a respected parish priest.

Jaws moved from the house even before I did and returned to Croatia, months before the terrible war broke out there.

The evening after my arrest, I collected the religious objects Marcello had found and loaded them on my motorbike, then drove through the bitter night air to the tiny village of Fonterutoli. I turned onto a very narrow side road that took me past a breathtakingly beautiful cypress forest, its rich evergreen hues piercing the smoky gray winter murk like a sense of hope. I then drove through a field—which called for a bit of skill to avoid falling or sinking into the deep, cold mud. Once across, I found myself at an abandoned farmhouse, its roof caved in but its walls still strong and sturdy. I paused to admire it as I skirted around.

Behind the house I got back onto a secondary road, then cut into a chestnut forest where thousands of prickly shells were strewn about with the rotting leaves, producing an acrid but pleasant earthy aroma.

Close to the bottom of a hill, I came to a tiny cemetery that contained no more than thirty tombstones, each for one of the souls who had lived in the few houses attached to the church of San Leonardo, now a shambles. The fifteenth-century structure had once been a presbytery, and in later times hosted several generations of the farmers who worked the surrounding fields. It was abandoned after the war, like so much of the Chianti countryside, and was now being slowly reclaimed by nature. The church had two palm trees, rarities at such latitudes, one on each side of the entrance, like sentries on duty.

Inside the church, I was impressed to see many statues and paintings, obviously covered in dust, but still intact. Even the wooden benches remained in place. I walked behind the altar and entered the little sacristy; I could hear the wind howling outside, and occasionally a gust would sweep through the broken windows.

I opened the cupboard and delicately replaced the sacred objects Marcello had taken away. I then returned to my Ducati and rode back home, thinking how beautiful San Leonardo would be were it ever to be restored.

5:12 P.M.

I descend from my perch high on the oak tree but, before I turn onto the path that leads to the village, I decide on a small diversion. I'm curious to see if by any chance my friend the *maestro* is camped with Martina at his usual spot. Since the *carabinieri* confiscated his driver's license for drinking and driving last year, he's been parked in a small clearing surrounded by a bush of bright yellow Spanish broom.

I head for the clearing—originally made by some local wild boar hunters to accommodate a wooden shed to shelter them during the long autumn rainfalls, and also to store the benches and tables they used when they gathered to grill monstrous numbers of sausages and quaff immoral quantities of Tuscan red. I have always been intrigued by the boar hunters; they seem for the most part average guys whose devotion to hunting is more an excuse to spend days on end with their buddies, away from their nagging wives.

Often when I drive by the forests I'll come across one of their shooting parties; they hunt down their prey in packs of thirty or forty. I'm always amused by the swarm of polished, brand-new giant SUVs and four-wheel drives parked on the roadsides, vehicles that are taken from their garages only for these rare events. Many of these also have trailer hitches—the hunters all own packs of expensive pedigreed hounds kept penned in small cages most of the year, and transporting the dogs anywhere requires a sizable trailer.

Of course we are in Italy where even the hunters have to be stylish, so they sport the latest and most expensive hunting gear. Many look as though they've been dressed by the more prestigious Milanese fashion designers. Their weapons are invariably the best Italian-made Beretta rifles, produced in Brescia in northern Italy. And to stay in touch when scattered deep in the woods, they use the most powerful and sophisticated high-tech walkie-talkies and cell phones. I doubt the Italian Ministry of Defense spends as much to defend our borders.

The hunters spend their days downing wine, smoking like chimneys, swearing like sailors, and laughing riotously over the latest dirty jokes. One thing that I've learned is that a wild boar hunter, if encountered one-on-one, is usually a charmingly ordinary Tuscan man; but group him with his companions and he'll fall victim to what I call the Neanderthal syndrome, transforming himself into the most brutal, unpleasant rogue possible. I've learned never to argue with them. What frightens me the most is that when they see the blood of the unfortunate animals they have slain, they become downright savage, their eyes lighting up with primitive excitement.

Then when they return home, drenched in blood and wine, they take a shower and as if by magic return to their everyday roles in society: the hospital administrator, the lawyer, the bank manager, whatever.

I turn onto the gravel road. Immediately beyond the bush of Spanish broom I spot what I was hoping to find: a 1970s-era orange Volkswagen van. The *maestro* is in! . . .

The Maestro

As usual, the *maestro*'s van has various pots of rosemary and thyme strewn across its roof and hood, and the scent of the herbs fills my nostrils as I knock on the cabin door.

I hear music coming from within, but no reply, so I try again. Still the notes of the legendary Italian rock group Premiata Forneria Marconi gently waft through the door, but there's no sign of the *maestro*. I knock yet again and call out his name, and suddenly a reply comes from right behind me. "Dario, *urka*," he says, using his favorite expression.

I whirl around to find him holding a bunch of wild asparagus in his right hand, in his left a roll of toilet paper. "I was busy—"

"Picking asparagus, *maestro*?" I interrupt.

He shakes his head. "Guess again," he says, gently shaking the roll of toilet paper. "*Urka*, I think I need to go to the optometrist," he adds.

"What for? It seems your eyesight is keen, judging by the amount of asparagus you found."

"No, it's for the other reason," he replies, again gently shaking the toilet roll. "I would like to know why is it, when I evacuate, my eyes water so much, *urka*!"

We both burst into laughter. The *maestro* hasn't changed. "Come inside. Martina will be happy to have you, Dario! I want to know about your trip to the United States, and I have a great red wine to spare."

I gulp at this, because despite his many other virtues the *maestro* is no wine expert. Actually, I would classify him more a wine masochist: The worse the wine, the more he seems to appreciate it. As if to underline my point, minutes later I'm sitting in his camper trying to think where I might secretly empty the little plastic cup of vinegar he's poured me. The only thing it might be good for is to dress a salad.

I met the *maestro* many years ago when my job as a tour guide had yet to take off, and so to make extra money I decided to give private English lessons. I put a small ad in the local paper:

> *English instructor, mother tongue, imparts lessons at modest prices in your home.*

A few days later I picked up the phone and a guttural voice said, "I would like to talk to the woman who teaches English."

A bit perplexed, I replied that as a matter of fact I was the instructor, and I was a man.

"*Urka,*" was the response; "then why do I read 'mother tongue'?"

When I realized he wasn't joking, I was speechless for a moment; then I explained the significance of the phrase *mother tongue*. He seemed satisfied, and said he was willing to give it a try. He told me he lived in a camper that could be found, this week anyway, in a certain parking lot in Radda in Chianti, and that he and Martina would be looking forward to meeting me.

On the day appointed for our first lesson I drove out to meet him. When I saw his camper, with a Jolly Roger pirate flag waving from the roof, I was a bit perplexed. I knocked on the door and was greeted by a tiny, puffy little man, his body shaped like a demijohn cork. Erupting from his head was a mass of curly black hair, so wide and wild that I wondered how, when he showered, the water managed to get past that fibrous mop to reach the rest of him. He wore a dark black beard that covered most of his face. His eyes were of a lively hazelnut color and had a curiously Oriental slant. His eyebrows were very thick, the right one interrupted by a small scar. He wore a pair of mauve shorts and a short-sleeved Hawaiian shirt. His legs and arms were completely covered by a jungle of black hair.

Billowing from the camper was the unmistakable stench of tripe, and as he led me inside I could see on the stove that he had been cooking giblets: livers, hearts, kidneys, brains, lungs, and some I couldn't identify.

He asked me to sit, produced a cheap plastic bottle, and poured me a white wine—according to him the nectar of Bacchus. I took a small sip, and if I'd had a chance I would have spit it out the window. I had to be polite, though, so I smiled and said it was excellent.

I learned that my new student was known in the hills as *il maestro,* for a number of reasons: He had been a teacher in the local elementary school, he was an amateur abstract painter, he created jewelry from pinecones (some of which he wore around his neck), and he had invented all kinds of curious devices. He showed me his pride and joy: a small battery-operated wooden contraption that, when he set a wineglass on it and pressed the ON button, started gently spinning around and around. "This way you don't have to turn the goblet during wine tasting," he proudly explained. "Is it not a great invention?"

I thought it was the most useless thing I had seen in my life (after alcohol-free beer), but kept the comment to myself. "If I manage to get it patented, I will be a very wealthy man," he said, beaming.

I couldn't pinpoint his age; I guessed him to be in his late forties, but I might have been wrong. Certainly his ardor for women was that of a younger man. He said he needed to learn English because he'd fallen in love with a woman from Idaho and wanted to go and visit her in the summer. He wouldn't fly, of course, the idea terrified him, and at any rate he wouldn't leave Martina behind. He explained that he had a friend at the port of Livorno who could get both him and his beloved vehicle onto a cargo ship headed for the United States. It was only at this moment that I realized Martina was not some woman who could show up at any moment, but was in fact the camper I was sitting in.

For some reason, the only thing he could say in English was "nevertheless," which I must admit he was capable of pronouncing in an admirable upper-class British accent. I went once a week to teach him, with scant results. In those days he would regularly move around the Chianti hills, and it seemed each week I would meet him in a new location. Sometimes he would park Martina in Gaiole, other times Radda or Castellina, or even Castelnuovo.

Every time I entered the van, the air was thick with the same gamey aroma of innards. I soon learned that he got them directly at the slaughterhouse, free of charge, and that they formed his main (and probably only) source of nutrition. He also never failed to pour me some indefinable brew he had the courage to call wine, and would even waste his time decanting it while trying to convince me of its virtues.

He had a hard time concentrating or even paying attention to the lessons, and after a few weeks I realized he would never learn anything; it was hopeless. Once when I was explaining the proper use of the present tense of the verb *to go*, he interrupted.

Staring at Martina's roof, he said, "*Urka,* Dario, you know at my age I've learned ugly women don't exist, it's all a matter of the amount of wine that you drink!" I was momentarily speechless, but admitted to myself the man did have a point.

I grew very fond of him, despite my virtually nonexistent job satisfaction. One day before our usual lesson, I filled up a Veuve Clicquot bottle I had emptied the night before with the cheapest fizzy, crappy wine I could find at the local market. I presented it to the *maestro* when I arrived. He opened it, poured some into a red plastic cup, then took a sip, and immediately arched his thick black eyebrows in delight. "*Urka!* When it comes to wine, the French are definitely the masters."

Three months later he finally realized that he was wasting his money on our once-a-week lessons. He looked at me earnestly with his little eyes narrowed and said, "Honestly, Dario, what do you think is the best way to learn English?"

Without hesitation I recommended immersing himself in the language—say, by going to England and living for a time with an English family. When I returned the following week, I found the camper without the flag on the roof, and the herbs he had planted were unusually dry; also I couldn't hear any music or—amazingly—smell any tripe.

As I was peering in the windows, an old man walking a dog approached me and said, "Are you Dario?" I nodded, and he handed me an envelope, which contained a note from the *maestro:* He had gone to Coventry in England to learn the language! He had found a family who agreed to host him in exchange for his help in their restaurant. He also apologized for not having called me, but he thought I might have talked him out of leaving.

So the *maestro,* my crazy, *simpatico* pupil, had gone to England—to Coventry of all places; incredible! He had obviously taken my advice quite seriously.

He returned nine months later, so excited that he called me from the public phone at a local bar and asked if we could meet immediately. I happily consented and drove my motorbike to Radda, where I found him pouring a glass of oxidized wine from a bottle with a tattered label into two glasses. Dante the barman later told me that the bottle wasn't for sale and had been sitting on a high shelf under the rays of sun for years, but the *maestro* had been so insistent on having it that he'd taken it down and given it to him.

"*Urka, Dario!*" the *maestro* cried when I walked in. As we embraced, he said, "*¿Qué tal, todo bien?*"

I was taken aback by his use of Spanish, having expected a torrent of English. But before I could inquire, he plunged excitedly into his narrative.

He told me in lavish detail how he had hitchhiked all the way to England, except for taking the ferry from the north of France. In Coventry he had been hosted by a wonderful family. He had washed the dishes in their restaurant in exchange for a bedroom and meals and had learned their language perfectly. The irony was that they were from Mexico and owned a Mexican restaurant, and that everyone spoke Spanish; now so did the *maestro,* quite fluently. "So your immersion theory was correct, Dario," he said, pleased.

"Great," I replied, "right advice, wrong language. You're the only person I ever met who went to England to learn English and came back speaking Spanish. Congratulations, *maestro,*" I said, adding "*Urka!*" for good measure.

I soon realized that having an English mother tongue wasn't enough to qualify me as an English teacher. My other two pupils both failed their exams, and so I gave it up. I was happy, though, to have met the *maestro,* and as he sits now listening attentively as I describe my experiences in America, I feel a warm glow of friendship. Or it might be the warmth of burgeoning indigestion from the foul wine with which he keeps refilling my glass, interjecting as he does so, *"Urka, Dario! Urka!"*

5:48 P.M.

After leaving the *maestro,* I continue my walk and enter an impeccably tended vineyard. The weeds have been pulled, uncovering the rocky terrain. Again, I am amazed that in this unforgiving soil, vines flourish and produce in just a few short months those juicy grapes that through the alchemy of fermentation transform into Chianti Classico; such are the miracles of nature.

The view of the Sangiovese vineyard causes me suddenly to thirst for a nice glass of red, so I decide to stop for a drink in the village. As I descend the steep hill, I hear the frogs croaking in a small reservoir in the distance, and the softly tinkling bells of grazing sheep in a nearby field.

Nearby, a dogwood is ready to bloom; even closer, a manna ash is already budding. I spot a cherry tree that soon will be bearing its juicy red fruits. I will certainly be back to collect them.

As I am about to enter the village, I see in the distance Clara chatting to her friend Gina, who has come to visit her from a neighboring village. They are two of my dearest friends. A wave of affection washes over me . . .

One of my favorite pastimes has always been listening to the stories of my village elders. Today many of these people are gone. Not only am I one of the few custodians of the personal lore and local history they bequeathed me, but their influence has been fundamental for the development of my career as well—for the more I understand of this region and its ways, the better I'm able to convey it to others.

I have always envied the older generations. While well aware of how hard their lives must have been, I can't help thinking they had the chance to live in the fullest sense, rather than merely exist. They were born in virtually a different dimension, a smaller, simpler world of community and camaraderie, far from our fast-paced, high-tech global village. From their beginnings, in a world without electricity or motorized transportation, they saw the invention (and subsequent invasion) of television and with it the full barreling stampede of modernity. If something was lost, they know what it was; and they are willing to tell me.

I find it pleasant to walk to the local tobacco store at certain hours, knowing I will encounter the same group of elderly ladies seated on the bench outside, basking in the warm sun and gossiping about the people passing by. They are always willing to share their disquisitions with others, and with patience and a little bit of flattery they can be prompted to open up their hearts and memories.

Clara and Gina in particular have much to say about the war years, when the retreating German army occupied my village of Vagliagli. Clara is an expansive character. Despite her age and her simple background—and hip problems so serious she requires the aid of two walking sticks—she is very much into fashion; her wardrobe is filled with colorful clothes, bizarre-looking hats, and the latest shoes. She always sports a thick layer of makeup and somewhat alarming shades of lipstick.

I enjoy picking her up and taking her out to lunch with Gina, who is about as different from Clara as it's possible to be. Much more a country type, she usually wears simple farmer's overalls. She's fit and full of energy, so much so that it seems that nothing can stop her. She still wakes up at four in the morning, collects the fresh eggs her hens have laid around her property, and then prepares the incredible homemade ravioli that her daughter will serve in her restaurant that night.

Whenever I drive Clara to Gina's, she sits beside me chatting away, filling the vehicle with some expensive, sweet, heavy perfume that masks all the odors the van has acquired in its many escapades better than any modern *arbre magique*. In autumn she will sometimes suddenly order me to halt and get out of the car, then from her lowered window direct me through the brush to where she has detected some giant porcini mushroom. I have no idea how she knows that in that very spot a precious bolus has grown, especially since often they are buried beneath heaps of leaves and invisible to the naked eye. If I ask her, she just laughs, touches the point of her nose with her heavily beringed finger, and says, "*Segreto.*" Top secret.

My favorite wartime story, which she has told me several times, goes back to 1944. Her family was very poor, and the long fighting had deprived them of even a guaranteed daily meal. Despite this, her father, to whom she was very attached, secretly asked a local tailor to make a summer dress for her birthday. It was an extraordinary gift, and Clara realized that her father had deprived himself of many slices of bread to pay for it.

She can still vividly remember the day her parents gave her the gift and the joy she felt in wearing that simple, summery, flower-print dress. She danced on the table with her uncle playing the accordion, her relatives clapping to the rhythm.

Unfortunately, this impromptu party was interrupted by a messenger who brought the news that the Germans were suffering severe setbacks and were rapidly retreating; in a few hours they would reach the village. This meant the risk of pillage and vandalism by the angry, defeated soldiers. The night that followed was terrible. Artillery fire grew progressively louder, which meant that the Allies were close by; that gave the villagers hope. But it was also possible that the invading Germans would simply blow up the whole village. Clara's first thoughts went to her brand-new dress. Her father told her to hand it to him; he would hide it in a safe place no German would ever discover.

Around 2:00 A.M. the family heard the German troops finally enter the village. They forced the door of the house open and three blond, blue-eyed, desperate young men burst in, shouting in German. Their uniforms were torn and tattered, and Clara remembers the bitter stench of sweat that immediately filled the room. It was clear that they were starving.

Clara's father set out a flask of wine, a loaf of bread, and a lump of salami that the Germans wolfed down in seconds. They then started emptying the cupboards in search of more; they overturned furniture while the family, clinging together, observed the scene with their heads bowed low in fear, not daring to protest. Clara cried in silence, hanging on to her father's coat until the poor man was pried away from her, taken outside, and beaten up by the drunken soldiers. Among Clara's worst memories are hearing those same screams coming from many of the neighbors.

Most of the village, though, was empty, for many of the inhabitants had fled to the nearby woods. The soldiers grabbed everything in sight and started to fill up their trucks. After a few terrifying hours, they finally left, heading north.

The war was over. The following morning, just as the cock crowed, the Allies arrived and the priest starting ringing the church bells in joy. The inhabitants who had been in hiding returned, and that evening a gigantic improvised feast was held in the square. This was a great opportunity for Clara to wear and show off her new dress. Her father, who had fortunately come away from his beating bearing only bruises, took her hand and led her to the backyard. Grabbing a shovel, he started digging up a pile of manure. The dress appeared at the bottom of the heap; it had been saved!

When Clara first told me this story, she looked at me and said, "You know, Dario, it smelled of shit, but who cared, I washed it in the stream and wore it anyway. And I will never be able to thank my father enough for that gift. The odor never went away, but even today, every time I smell manure it reminds me of freedom!"

Gina has a different way of telling her stories. She is so expressive, and gestures so often, that it almost seems as if she is miming the entire scene. She constantly runs the palm of her hands over her snow-white hair and at the end of each phrase exclaims "*Davvero! Mamma mia!*"

One evening I went to visit her and found her busy chopping firewood for the long winter to come. I watched in awe as this eighty-year-old woman plunged an ax through the logs as easily as she might slice a knife through a stick of butter. Such is her sheer strength that I'd bet on her today to beat a fit male half her age in an arm-wrestling competition.

Afterward, she invited me indoors, where she gave me a glass of her homemade *vin santo* and shared with me one of her own wartime reminiscences. Her village had been occupied by a small group of German soldiers. They weren't quite as nasty as she'd heard other German troops were, except for the sergeant in charge, who was always hungry and keen on drinking her precious *vin santo*. "*Mamma mia, Dario*," she exclaimed, clasping her forehead, "he finished off an entire barrel in just a few days—*davvero*!"

The Allies were very close, and nearby villages were being rapidly liberated. The French had a small group of Moroccan soldiers who were often sent as advance scouts to check out the German positions. "*Mamma mia*," she said with a hoot of laughter, "they would have sex with any animal in sight, leaving the women untouched because the French officers would shoot them if they even touched us! *Davvero*, Dario, *davvero*, these men calmed their boiling spirits by screwing our sheep, our donkeys, our *anything*!" Her laughter echoed down the valley.

The Moroccans also invented a macabre game: They would assault the German guards and, after killing them, cut off their ears. "At the end of the day," Gina explained, "the one who produced the most ears was awarded with an extra portion of soup. *Davvero*, Dario, *mamma mia*!" Another roar of hearty laughter. "Now, my father was a tough, brave man, Dario, and early one morning while walking down to the creek to wash he saw a dead German soldier in the ravine. His ears had been cut off, so my father realized that some Moroccan must be close by. He lowered himself and crouched down and saw a Moroccan soldier washing off bloodstains in the river. He also noticed that the poor German soldier had a pack of cigarettes in his front pocket. My father was a great smoker and this pleasure had been hindered by the wartime shortages. He was very eager to get those cigarettes, and he knew the Moroccan wasn't going to leave them there. So while the Moroccan was washing, he boldly crawled over to the dead soldier—who had already attracted a swarm of flies—and managed to snatch the cigarettes and get away before the Moroccan noticed him.

"The packet, though, was completely drenched in blood, and so when he got home, he delicately pulled them out one by one with his large fingers, making sure not to damage them, and lined them up along the wall under the sun. Then, patiently, he waited a few hours for the sun to dry them out. And when they were dry he smoked them all, one after the other; as soon as he finished one, he lit the next. He finished the whole pack in just a couple of hours, *mamma mia*!

"I observed him from the window, puffing away. He would inhale slowly, filling his lungs with smoke with such a look of satisfaction, I can't describe the pleasure my papa was feeling that moment. To see him so happy after years of suffering filled my heart with joy. I think I counted forty cigarettes in all, or even more, but he deserved it.

"The day before the liberation, the German sergeant, while completely drunk, put his foot on a land mine that he himself had ordered to be buried in an empty field right over there—" She pointed toward what is now the village parking lot. "He lost his leg, and I can still remember the screams of agony when he was loaded on a truck and was taken away, along with the other soldiers. *Dario, mamma mia! Mamma . . . mia.*" She shook her head in amazement. "Can you imagine that just ten years ago I was preparing some sandwiches in my bar when a big black Mercedes pulled up in the square, and out came an old man with a peg leg accompanied by what I figured were his children. I recognized him immediately: It was the old sergeant. I handed him a glass of *vin santo*, and the old man took it with a trembling hand and smiled. I looked at him and said, '*Figlio di puttana!* You son of a bitch, you remember my *vin santo*, eh?' He obviously couldn't understand me but I persisted, saying, 'I know you lost your leg here, have you come back to see if you can find it?'" Gina looked at me, her eyes swollen with tears. "*Davvero*, Dario! I swear, those were my words." She then burst into a peal of laughter, showing all her gold-capped teeth. "*Mamma mia*," she said at last, clapping her hands. She ended her story by saying that she invited the old man to dinner, and I could only think, *Good old Gina*.

Driving back that evening on the deserted roads that separate Gina's village from mine, I bask in the serenity of my hills, the peaceful ambience, the power these landscapes have to fill my soul with joy and peace. I still find it hard to believe that anyone can cultivate hateful feelings here, in the face of such beauty.

6:27 P.M.

I pass the local *carabinieri* station. Its insignia is partly covered by wisteria vine, and the last violets and primroses are drying in the adjacent uncultivated field. The village kids are playing soccer in the small playground next to the village clubhouse. Suddenly the ball comes flying through the air and lands at my feet. "Will you kick it back?" the ten-year-old Domenico cries out.

"Only if I can play, too," I reply.

I roll up my sleeves, leap onto the playing field, and find myself kicking the ball around with the youngsters. I'm a little out of practice, but then that never stopped me before . . .

The Soccer Tournament

A couple of years ago I had just returned from a day's tour and was reflecting on how delightful my two clients had been. Cristina was already home and was busy pulling the withering flowers from the terra-cotta pots on the windowsill. I'd never liked this chore, because it means winter was nigh. Cristina smiled and kissed me on the cheek, revealing all of her beauty in the late-autumn light.

My contemplation of her sweetness was interrupted by the buzz of my cell phone. It was my friend Andrea calling. "*Ehilà*, Dario, how's life? Everything under control?" he said, using one of his characteristic expressions. I said yes, everything was under control, and he continued: "Listen, I have some exciting news. Leo has re-formed the team and entered us for the annual seven-a-side soccer tournament at Vico Alto—"

Before he could get out another word, I interrupted with an incredulous "*What?*

. . . But—we quit playing ten years ago. We don't stand a chance! Why did he do this?"

"We're meeting at his house tonight," Andrea said. "I expect we'll find out then. Anyway, you'd better show up—we need a right wing."

Cristina shook her head when I put down the receiver, and said, "Will you ever grow up?" I wanted to tell her, *I thought I had . . .*

After dinner I jumped into my van and drove the potholed road that leads to the village of Quercegrossa. Leo was in the garage with the other team members drinking beer straight from the bottle. The room was exactly the same as when we were teenagers, the walls covered with posters of soccer stars of that era, the window sill filled with the trophies we'd won in past tournaments.

My old friends greeted me with hugs and high fives, then handed me both a stool and a Moretti beer. When our reunion greetings were concluded, Leo explained that he had signed us up for the tournament because it was the tenth anniversary of our last one. "But Leo," Andrea said while emptying his second bottle of beer, "we quit after that tournament because we got thrashed and realized it was time to retire. We can't go back after ten *more* years. We'll be humiliated."

Leo, however, seemed serenely confident. He said, "The tournament's very short—just two groups of four teams. The first two meet for the semifinals, and then the finals. Plus, since we haven't trained for such a long time, we must be well rested, with plenty of energy to expend. And we're all in our forties—our secret weapon will be experience! Anyway, I think we should have a shot, and . . . what can I tell you, *I want that cup!*" Buoyed by his optimism, we all stood and raised our bottles, shouting, "*Here's to the cup!*"

And then we began clinking. I first banged my bottle against Leo's, and he rewarded me with a big smile. He was a very nice chap, a total nonconformist, with memberships in Amnesty International, the World Wildlife Fund, Save the Planet, Friends of Guatemala, the Anti-Vivisectionist League, and many other progressive social and environmental organizations. He was less ambitious on a personal scale; he never managed to get a driver's license and worked in the children's department of a local hospital; his wife was about his size, and they had a fifteen-year-old son.

In his youth he had been a decent player; he was very fast and had a natural gift for scoring. He had since passed 260 pounds and was missing a few teeth. He still wore his hair in a ponytail, but it was now snowy white. He was a very pleasant man and, despite a tough-guy act, wouldn't hurt a fly.

The next bottle I clinked was that of Andrea Giubbolini—Andrea the insurance executive with whom I lunched so memorably years before. Then I turned to toast Luciano, our goalkeeper, a shy and gentle fellow. He was happily married and worked for an organization providing recovery services to drug addicts. He had a passion for fast cars and participated in rally races, as well as having once been a skilled fencer.

Now I found myself bottle-to-bottle with Beppe. I hadn't seen him for a long while, but I vividly recalled his eventful history. In his twenties he had had many problems with the law: He became a drug addict, was arrested for burglarizing apartments, spent some time in jail, and then went through detox in Luciano's clinic. Now he was working with his brother as a bricklayer, had gotten married, and seemed to have solved his problems.

Beppe was our left back defender; the right back was Marruga, the policeman who had arrested him. I saluted him now, and again marveled at his choice of career—out of all the possibilities open to him, I would never have imagined him becoming a defender of the law. After all, as a teenager he had been the comsummate delinquent, even getting himself expelled from school. But he had acquitted himself honorably on the police force. Marruga had been married but was now divorced.

The sixth member of the team, whose bottle mine now met, was Berto, the owner of a local pub. Single and a night animal, he utterly refused to accept his age and could often be found dancing in local discos with teenagers until very early in the morning. He kept his hair very long and uncombed and his face unshaven; this, combined with his strong, sturdy frame and general scruffiness, had earned him the nickname Neanderthal. Despite his unhealthy habits he was still apparently a very good player—reportedly our ace.

Next were the twins, Sandro and Gigi. They were identical, both pale as ghosts, and had an uncanny habit of speaking in unison. Both worked in the local bank. When one was sick so was the other; when one found a girlfriend, so did the other;

when one scored, so did his twin. They were very small framed and fast, and were supposed to play midfield. Both single, they lived with their parents on a vineyard.

I turned to clink bottles with the local butcher, Cocco. He was a quiet sort, another divorcé, and I had to be very careful when talking to him because his reactions were unpredictable. Perhaps as a result, I had never had a friendly relationship with him. He was a defender who would kick whoever dribbled past him. His face was pockmarked, making his angelic curly blond hair look totally out of place.

The last in the garage was Beniamino, a disabled boy who lived close to Leo and whom Leo kept under his wing. Given his age he hadn't participated in our past tournaments; with his mental and physical impairments he'd serve now only as our mascot. We all loved him for his purity and innocence, and we strove to give him a feeling of worth.

Now that we had finished our toasts, we sat back down on our stools and listened to Leo, who was obviously acting as player, coach, and manager of the team.

"We have a sponsor," he said, "and they've paid for our shirts." He unfolded one from a large pile he had stacked on a wicker chair next to him. On the front it read:

BAR RESTAURANT PIZZERIA EXTRAMOENIA

EXIT SIENA WEST

SPECIALTY FRIED FROG LEGS

"We are *not* going to play with those shirts," declared Andrea. "We'll look ridiculous."

"Come on," said Leo calmingly, "who really cares what the name of the team is? They've been kind enough to give us the shirts, and if we win the tournament they'll also give us dinner." That seemed to silence any grumbling, at least for the moment, so Leo continued. "The games commence on Sunday morning. We'll meet at the usual bar at seven thirty; kickoff is an hour later, so I want you all to be punctual."

Someone asked about training, and Leo said it would only make us tired. So again we raised our bottles, then said good night.

On the way home I thought that Leo may have been feeling nostalgia for the past and had organized the team simply as an excuse to reconnect with old friends. Still, the idea wasn't necessarily a bad one . . . My mind started to wander, as I tried to remember where my soccer boots might be, and I nearly ran over a badger on the dirt road.

When I returned I found Cristina sound asleep. I tucked the blankets around her and crouched in close, taking in her warmth. That night I dreamed of scoring the winning goal in the European Champions League final.

Come Sunday morning I had no trouble getting out of bed early. In fact, I was eager for the day—even though the weather was cold and rainy.

I drove to the meeting place and was rather surprised to find Leo and Andrea eating cream doughnuts, accompanied not by a cappuccino but by a beer. Luciano, his former patient Beppe, and Marruga were there as well as Beniamino. They all greeted me, and we waited together for the others to turn up.

And waited.

And *waited.*

After half an hour we gave up and drove to the field without them. The other team was already warming up on the field; they were all fit and athletic, the oldest of them looking no more than twenty-five, and they had at least thirteen players to our seven. That meant that they could change six players during the match. We were getting nervous, as it seemed that nobody else was likely to turn up, meaning we had no subs and Beniamino would have to play from the very first minute.

The locker rooms were filthy and damp—perfect for cultivating mushrooms, I thought—and it was still raining and very cold. To make things even worse, we now discovered that our shirts were sleeveless.

The referee entered the locker room for his briefing, and Leo handed him the list of players, explaining that some others might turn up later.

"Have a good game," said the referee. "Kickoff is in ten minutes."

We went on to the field to warm up a bit, and Leo assigned us positions: Luciano in goal, left-back Beppe, fullback Andrea, right-back Marruga, with Beniamino in the center of the field. I was told to play center forward with Leo.

"Remember, we have to base our game on *experience*," he said now, trying to rev us up. "The Montalcino Tigers are just a bunch of green kids. Let's just play the ball with class and we can beat them."

The referee blew his whistle again and called the captains to midfield—which, due to the continuing rain, was a swamp of mud. The captains exchanged a handshake, then Leo won the toss and chose the right-hand side of the field for the first half.

The Montalcino Tigers were to kick off. "For the Montalcino Tigers, *hip hip hurrah*," we shouted in traditional good sportsmanship. The Tigers responded with, "For Bar Restaurant Pizzeria Extramoenia exit Siena West specialty fried frog legs, *hip hip hurrah*." Some of them were visibly struggling not to laugh.

The game commenced. Our opponents passed the ball to their right wing; he dribbled past Beniamino, who tripped and fell in a puddle. The Tiger avoided Marruga's tackle and crossed the ball in the center; the forward opposed by Andrea towered over him and headed the ball. Luciano made a spectacular dive but couldn't prevent the goal, and we were already one down. Leo was furious! He started shouting, "*Wake up!* How can we get a goal against us after *ten seconds*? Maybe I should call the *Guinness Book of Records*! Come on, *come on*!"

The jubilant Tigers embraced their forward while we returned to the center. Leo passed me the ball and I kicked it back to Marruga, but it got stuck in the mud. Immediately a Tiger pounced on it, flicked it into the air, then trapped it with his chest and sent it spiraling to their wing—this time on the left. This wing made a diagonal run toward the goal, and Beppe blocked him—too late, as his opponent took an incredible shot and sent the ball flying into the back of the net.

Luciano didn't even have time to realize what had happened. Two minutes, and we were two down. "Oh my God," Leo cried, "what the hell are we doing? This is humiliating! *Experience*, remember experience? Pull yourselves together!"

After five minutes they scored again. This time Leo decided the only thing to do was to close ranks in front of our goalkeeper to avoid the worst, and as soon as we had intercepted the ball to kick it over the fence.

But it was hopeless. Every time they drove forward they were relentless, and they had no pity. At the end of the first half, the score was eloquent. Montalcino Tigers: 7, Bar Restaurant Pizzeria Extramoenia exit Siena West specialty fried frog legs: 0.

Fortunately there were very few spectators due to the foul weather and the early hour. But that was small comfort as we entered the locker room with our heads hung low. We were all exhausted, sweaty, and panting, and to make things worse we had no substitutes. None of our absent teammates had yet shown up.

Leo closed the door, kicked the bench, opened a Moretti beer, and sank his head into his palms in silence. We could hear the Tigers next door laughing and cheering, probably sipping cups of hot tea.

At that moment the door opened, and in came Berto and Cocco! "Hey, lads," Berto said jovially while stripping off his shirt, "sorry we're late, we were at an after-hours disco party." Judging by their movements, I was pretty sure they were high on something.

"You guys look like you're just back from a funeral," Berto continued as he suited up. Andrea explained them the situation. They said, "Okay, we'll see if we can make things less worse."

The second half started with Berto in place of Beniamino and Cocco in the center of the defense in place of Andrea, who was very happy to leave the field. The clock started. I kicked off and advanced a few yards, then passed the ball to Berto; he passed an opponent—then a second, a third, a fourth! He slipped the ball through the fullback's legs and shot it into the net. Score!

Three minutes later Berto shot from 20 yards and scored again. Clearly the club drugs were still circulating; I thought how fortunate it was that at this level we didn't have anti-doping controls.

The Tigers, shocked by our sudden comeback, went on the attack. Their center forward, who had scored a hat trick in the first half, jumped Cocco, who kicked him from behind. The referee pulled out a yellow card and called out Cocco—"None of that, young man! One more move like that and you're off!"

The Tiger lobbed the ball into the center, and the center forward took a volley shot. Luciano, agile as a cat, leapt to his left and put the ball out of play. The left winger crossed the ball from the corner, and the center forward went for a header. Cocco raised his elbow and crashed it into his face; the forward fell into the mud holding his bleeding nose. Cocco sneered, *"That'll teach you!"* The referee waved the red card at him and sent him off.

One of the Tigers approached Cocco menacingly. I tried to block him, warning that the guy was dangerous, but he shoved me to the ground. Seeing this, Leo caught him by his collar and punched him in the face. Suddenly all the players invaded the field, while the referee blew his whistle furiously, ending the game.

The field was now a free-for-all saloon brawl. Marruga raced off, jumped into his car, and escaped; he knew the police would soon arrive, and he didn't want his colleagues to see him here. Cocco was surrounded by at least six furious young Tigers but managed to stay on his feet, returning every blow. I got a right fist in my eye and fell face-first in the mud. The referee tried without success to end the fight.

Minutes later we heard the sirens, and a police car and an ambulance careened onto the scene. Their presence calmed us all down. As paramedics loaded the broken-nosed center forward onto a stretcher, we were escorted back to the locker room, where the referee declared that the game had been suspended due to the disgraceful behavior of Cocco, who was banned from the tournament. The rules in this case were that the Tigers were declared the winners, 3–0, which was of course better than the 7–2 we'd been facing earlier.

I could feel my eye swell up; I looked in the mirror and realized I had a shiner. I shrugged it off, and after the shower we went for lunch, drank an obscene quantity of wine, and ate tripe and steaks. Leo said, "If we play with the spirit of the second half, we can pass the first round."

When I got back home and Cristina saw me, she shook her head, laughed, and handed me some ice. "Dario, Dario, when will you grow up?"

The second game was played on a Wednesday evening after dinner. We were playing the team from the local Bar Vico Alto, a bunch of unemployed layabouts who had drawn the first game against the Prosecco Boys 1–1. This time there were a few hundred spectators, our entire team turned up, and Cocco—still disqualified—sat on the bench.

Leo said, "Luciano in goal, Beppe left, Andrea fullback, Marruga right, Dario and Berto in midfield, and I'll stay up front. The twins on the bench with Beniamino." He paused, then suddenly looked serious. "After our last game let's learn our lesson: We have to honor our tournament. Remember, if we win we have a chance of going through to the second round."

The game commenced. This time we were very careful not to allow an early goal. After ten minutes of attacks from the Bar Vico Alto, Berto—who seemed to be sober—jumped two defenders and crossed toward the center. Leo blocked the ball with his chest but had his back turned toward the goal. He raised the ball in the air and despite his massive bulk did a bicycle kick and fell heavily on his back. The crowd was speechless; he had scored a goal of rare beauty, something hardly ever seen even among the pros.

We all raced toward him, concerned he might be hurt, but he struggled to his feet. "Now," he said, still slightly winded, "it's all defense. Whenever we get the ball let's just kick it over the fence."

Bar Vico Alto attacked us relentlessly for the rest of the first half, but somehow we managed to keep the lead. In the locker room Leo sipped happily at his bottle of Moretti beer, but warned us to keep our concentration. We were close, very close to victory . . .

Alas, the second half was a total disaster. Berto had no energy left, I sprained my ankle and had to leave the field, and the twins who were sent in to replace us had no impact on the game. We lost 8–1. Despite our black mood, we stuck around to watch the Montalcino Tigers defeat our next opponents, the Prosecco Boys, 2–0. At this point the standings were:

Montalcino Tigers: 6 points
Bar Vico Alto: 4 points
Prosecco Boys: 1 point
Bar Restaurant Pizzeria Extramoenia exit Siena West specialty fried frog legs: 0 points

Mathematically, we were already out of the tournament, yet we still had a game to play. Leo appealed to our honor, urging us to respect the tournament and at least *try* to win the last game.

This time when I got back home, I could barely walk. Cristina looked at me and said, "Black eye, sprained ankle—what great trophy will you bring home next?" I told her I doubted I'd recover in time for the final game, and that we had no more chances of going to the next round anyway, and as far as I was concerned I was finished with soccer. I opened the trash can and threw my soccer boots inside.

On Friday evening I drove to the bar, where the team was discussing strategy before the last game. I was injured, Cocco was banned, and Luciano had to work. No goalie, then.

Leo walked up to a seemingly healthy young fellow who was leafing through a paper at the bar, explained the situation to him, and asked if he was willing to play for us. He looked up eagerly and said, "Sure!" Then he stood . . . and we realized that his legs had been crippled by polio.

Leo couldn't very well retract the offer without mortifying everyone, so we set off to the field under a cloud of impending doom.

This time Simone, the new player, took the goal; left-back Beppe; fullback Andrea; right-back Marruga; Sandro and Berto in midfield; Leo attacking; and on the bench Beniamino and Gigi, the other twin.

There was a fair-sized crowd in the stands, and many of them started taunting us because of our name, our previous scores, our handicapped goalkeeper, and the size of Leo's stomach—now distended by God knows how many liters of Moretti beer.

The field was in good shape, and the sky was full of stars. So there was a brief glimmer of hope . . . and then the game started.

Berto, whom we soon realized had only enough energy for one half, took a beautiful shot from the edge of the box after six minutes and scored. The Prosecco Boys drew even just before the end of the first half. In the second half Leo, who had by now had enough of being heckled by a spectator, snapped; he walked toward the stands, shouting, "Hey, your sister is good in bed, you know that? Don't take my word for it, just ask anybody on the team!" The heckler stood up and shouted back. Before things could deteriorate further, the referee pulled out the red card and sent Leo off.

But Leo didn't *go* off. He turned to the referee, said, "*Your* sister ain't bad, either," then stunned us all by pulling down his shorts and mooning the crowd, which was by now booing and throwing trash onto the field.

When Leo joined us on the bench, I thought of reminding him of his speech about "honoring the tournament," but seeing the look on his face I decided against it.

Berto was now exhausted and needed a substitute. We were one man short and our ace was on the bench with ten minutes to go. Andrea and the other defenders did a great job and the twins gave a hand, but in the last minute one of the opponents found himself alone in front of our goalie and was about to score—when Beppe tackled him from behind and sent him flying! Inevitably the referee sent Beppe off and ordered a penalty kick.

Blow, I thought, *we've lost again, Simone can't even move.* In the goal Simone wore a look of deep concentration while the enemy forward prepared to shoot. Finally he took a run and kicked the ball with all his might. Simone tripped on his right; he guessed the direction and by some fluke deflected the ball. The referee blew the whistle—game over. We hadn't lost!

That evening we all went for dinner at the sponsor's place to try the famous specialty frog legs. They didn't give us dinner on the house, as we hadn't won the tournament, but they did give us a generous discount. I was still in very bad shape. Well, everyone was, in one way or another. Yet the wine flowed, and the Moretti beer flowed, and while we hadn't recaptured the glory of our youth exactly, we laughed throughout the entire meal and far into the night.

7:37 P.M.

After I finish my soccer game with the kids, I realize that the village has filled with people. As I approach my favorite wine bar, Paolo greets me with a hug and offers to pour me a glass of his best. Next door the restaurant staff is taking delivery of a cart of firewood they'll use to grill meat that evening. Checco is the deliveryman; he's unmistakable, with his great height and his glasses thick as bottle bottoms. He dwarfs his tiny Filipino wife, who's giving him a hand unloading.

Marta and Eva—both in their late teens—are busy chatting on one of the benches, and I guess they are talking about boys. I notice, not for the first time, how pretty they are. Marta nervously bites the nails of one hand while twirling her hair with the forefinger of the other; Eva, more serene, gazes at her friend with her dizzying blue eyes, listening attentively.

Lucone sips on his usual can of ice-cold tea; he downs at least fifteen of these a day and is teased for it. In front of the bar, around a plastic table, Gnagno, Spadino, and Il Socio are drinking a Campari each, talking with great animation about either soccer or the upcoming Palio. A group of men sits under the oak tree smoking cigarettes and discussing the imminent village feast. In the small alley close to the bar, some women are busy knitting and deciding what to cook for their husbands for dinner.

I spot Pepita's old Mercedes parked in front of the food store; she's in her nineties, and legend has it she was the one who managed to convince the Nazis not to blow up the village in World War II.

Gregorio appears in his overalls and, judging by the bags he's toting, has just returned from his vegetable garden. He stops to give me a bunch of fresh fava beans, which I so love to eat raw with some pecorino cheese and red wine. Throughout the village we can hear little Giulia singing, and her father Cicala accompanying her on the keyboard. And here comes Giacomo, walking his big gray dog Gigio. Everyone stops to greet me and welcome me back.

It's good to be in my own environment I think as I walk back home. I enter my house just as it's getting dark, the sun setting behind the hills, the air turning chilly. I put on a sweater and fetch my sleeping bag from the cupboard, then stop over to ask my neighbor if he has a piece of bread to spare. He does. I slip it into my duffel bag along with a flashlight, a lighter, a piece of garlic, salt, a bottle of olive oil and one of wine, and a sturdy wine glass. I walk to the car and drive down the hill, to where the road suddenly narrows and the asphalt gives way to gravel.

I drive on a few miles more, then park in front of a chestnut forest and make my way through a hedge of thick blackberry. I can hear the wild boars happily snorting and rooting. I continue for a while longer, until it gets pitch dark, then turn on my flashlight. I'm at the foot of a hill where a small creek flows close to an abandoned mill. It's been years since I last visited this spot, and I'm heartened to find it exactly as I left it.

The sun has now set behind the hills but the moon is full

and bright, illuminating the valley with a pleasant silvery glow. The horizons of the hills are still perceivable. I trace the sloping lines that divide the hilltops from the infinite spatter of stars.

The sound of the running water in the Serchia creek acts as my soundtrack on this young night, and I can hear the first crickets, too—a sure sign that summer is nigh. The mill is abandoned, but in the dim light I can see furrows where a tractor has plowed the fields opposite; most likely someone from a nearby farm decided to make some hay to feed the prestigious *chianine* beef that is butchered and grilled, and served rare as *fiorentina* steaks in the local restaurants.

I lie down on the sleeping bag and look up at the stars. I'm not able to recognize the constellations, but that's fine; I really just want to enjoy the scenery.

The peace and quiet and the vastness of the sky all twine together to call forth memories. It's already been a day filled with memories, but in these waning hours I find I have room for one more, possibly the most intense . . .

Matteo

It was the beginning of June. I was fifteen years old, heading for school on the Number 8 bus that drops me off at the Agricultural Technical High School of Siena. The narrow bus was packed tight as sardines. My eye fell on a serious-looking young teenager standing gripping the rail. I felt immediately pity for him, as he had a pronounced hunchback.

Still, he was good looking. His hair was jet black, and he had emerald-green eyes set in a suntanned face. I watched him for a few moments, till suddenly he whirled and started yelling at a girl: "I felt that! I felt you touch me! What is it, do you have an exam today? Touch the hunchback for luck? . . . My God, it's the twentieth century, but some idiots still believe any ridiculous superstition . . ."

The girl immediately blushed and dozens of eyes fell on her in disgust. In a feeble voice she tried to deny that she had actually touched him, but clearly no one believed her. An old woman stood up and offered her seat to the boy, who accepted the kind offer.

At the next stop he stood up, and everyone made way to let him pass. He got off the bus accompanied by a wave of compassion. The doors were about to close again when I was caught by a sudden impulse; despite this not being my stop, I jumped out after him.

The boy entered a bar and I followed him. He slammed his right hand on the wooden counter and said, "A tear of red wine please," then headed toward the bathroom. I ordered a cup of *orzo* and leafed through the daily paper, skimming over the headlines.

A few minutes later the boy reappeared. To my surprise his hunchback had disappeared; he was walking erect. He started chatting with a beautiful girl, and when an old man walked by, the boy stood in his way, then snatched the man's hat from his head and waved it back and forth in the air, singing, "*One for you, one for me.*"

Everyone in the bar turned to observe the scene, laughing out loud. At first merely embarrassed, the old man soon lost his patience: "You young fool, you give that back!" Seconds later, the boy replaced the hat on the man's bald head, emptied his wine with one gulp, and exclaimed, "Excellent, this nectar!"

Then he kissed the girl on her lips, pulled some change from his pocket, deposited it on the counter, and left.

I followed him outside, got his attention, and asked him what had happened to his hunchback. Slyly he grinned, then patted his rucksack on his elbow and said, "It's right here." He extended his arm and said, "Matteo."

"Dario," I said, shaking his hand.

He asked me for a cigarette but I didn't have any. He went back into the bar—again, I followed—where he asked the woman behind the counter for a pack of Nordquists without filters. The woman, whose heavy makeup and cheap blond dye job couldn't hide her middle age, replied that she didn't have that brand.

"Okay," said Matteo, "I'll take one *with* filter."

"We don't have that, either," she replied.

Matteo was persistent. "Gallapaltos, then."

The woman scowled. "Never heard of it."

"Worsteins?"

"No."

"Julius mild?"

"Listen, boy," she said, clearly at the end of her rope, "I've never even heard of these brands. You're wasting my time."

He reached up boldly, pinched both her cheeks, and said, "*Signora,* this bar has *nothing.* Kindly hand me a pack of Marlboros."

The woman went red in the face; she was clearly ready to explode. She gave him the pack, then asked him to leave the premises and never return.

Once outside he stopped a sweet-faced old lady carrying some heavy shopping bags. He put his left wrist in front of his face and said very rapidly, "*Ti puzz il cul sai?*" Did you know your ass stinks? She put down her shopping bags, looked at her watch, and said, "It's eight forty-five, dear."

"Thank you," Matteo replied with the most angelic expression possible.

"So, Dario," he asked as he lit a cigarette, "what are you up to now?"

"Well, I should be going to school," I replied.

"You can always go tomorrow," he said. "Plus, I bet you already went yesterday." He smiled and winked. "Me, I'm about to go to a special place. Why not come along?"

He had a Vespa parked close by. It looked just like the ordinary Vespa 50cc thousands of Italian teenagers, including me, possessed in those years, except that it had two seats, front and back. It was also slightly dented and had no flanks covering the engine on the side, but apart from that it looked fine.

He kicked the pedal and the engine immediately growled loudly to life. "Jump on," he said. I leapt on the backseat, and he lurched the scooter forward, popping a wheelie so that I nearly fell off. We then took off like a shot, tearing down the street at impressive speed. Above the roar of the engine, he told me he'd modified the engine to 130cc.

We zoomed along a cypress-lined road that led back down to the old city walls. He had to slow down when we came up behind a lumbering truck, but Matteo clearly wasn't content to let someone else set his pace. He swerved to the left and began to pass the truck, but as soon as he did so, a bus came at us in the opposite lane. As the bus driver sounded his horn in alarm, Matteo shifted down a couple of gears, to my relief. Imagine my horror when, instead of falling back behind the truck, he lunged into third gear and zipped directly between truck and bus! "You're crazy!" I cried. "Slow down or you'll kill us both!"

"Have faith," he replied while sailing past a stop sign—mere moments before similarly ignoring a red traffic light.

Inevitably we heard the whistle of a traffic warden. Matteo ignored it as though it were the whistle of the wind. As I clung to him I thought that, apart from speeding, jumping red lights, riding a modified Vespa with an illegal passenger seat, and skipping school, everything was fine.

The situation escalated when we heard police sirens wailing behind us. Matteo remained unfazed; he tore through the ancient city gates and up a one-way street. But the police car remained on our tail, so halfway up the steep hill he abruptly turned right and went skittering down a flight of medieval steps, nearly knocking over an old man walking his Yorkshire terrier; he dodged just in time, then waved his fist angrily after us. I was genuinely scared and could feel my adrenaline coursing wildly through me. Still, we seemed to have lost the police car.

Suddenly we roared into the countryside. It was a warm day, and the poppy fields had attracted the first insects. Matteo slowed down as if enchanted by so much beauty. I realized that the boundless serenity out here, the warmth of the sun beating down on our heads, relaxed him.

We passed through a series of small hamlets until we reached the village of Brenna, where he crossed a stone bridge over a river and drove down a narrow, dusty, gravel side road. A few kilometers later he stopped and we got off the Vespa. He propped it on its stand, then opened a leather bag tied to the carrier and took out a small metal sign on which he had written *ATTENZIONE ALLE VIPERE!* BEWARE OF VIPERS! He tied this to a large oak tree, and said, "Nobody will come and disturb us."

"You're crazy," I said, meaning it, but we both started laughing. We descended a tiny goat path that led to the bottom of the valley.

During the walk we got better acquainted. I asked him about the hunchback scene I'd witnessed on the bus; he told me he'd seen a comedian do it in a movie and wanted to emulate him, to see what kind of reactions he could provoke. For the same reason, he amused himself inventing nonexistent brands of cigarettes to drive tobacconists crazy.

The hills were painted yellow with Spanish broom, and the flowers' heady perfume enveloped the valley. An endless variety of wild plants blossomed all around us, even in the rockiest fields: cornflowers, poppies, chamomile and more. We spotted a den and guessed it to be a badger's; we found and collected some very long and sharp porcupine quills

Minutes later we reached the river. After that year's abundant winter rainfalls, it was flowing rapidly. It seemed very deep; the bottom wasn't even visible. On the opposite bank a mother with two small children was playing on the pebble beach. This evidence that we were not alone seemed to disturb Matteo; he scowled, then looked at me with his sly green eyes and told me his plan for getting rid of them. I giggled. He took off his jeans and Fruit of the Loom T-shirt and dived into the water; seconds later he started screaming at the top of his lungs. The mother was startled and stood up to observe the scene, clasping her children's hands. Matteo waved his arms, crying for help. This was my cue to enter the scene: I jumped in the ice-cold water, swam toward him, and—with my hand under his chin as I had learned at a rescue course—dragged him onto the beach where the family had spread their towels. They stood back, looking on in alarm.

As I hovered over Matteo, the mother crept closer and asked politely if there was anything she could do. Matteo, in a feeble, anguished voice, explained that he had been bitten by a *tarallo*. "They're nasty beasts," he gasped, a terrible grimace on his face.

He beat his palm on his forehead. "The pain is unbearable!" He reached down and grasped his ankle. "*Signora,*" he said, "I suggest you take the kids away immediately. The *taralli* can be very dangerous. Normally they travel in packs; I was lucky to run into just one. But others might be lurking about."

The woman picked up her things and asked if Matteo would be okay. He nodded, saying that the pain would soon pass and then I could get him to First Aid. She turned and led her children away, then some yards on turned back and asked again the name of the animal that had attacked him. "*Tarallo,*" we replied in chorus. She nodded and hurried away.

Now we were really alone. We lay with our backs on the pebbles, congratulating ourselves on our nasty little ruse, and trying to think up a form our imaginary beast might take. When we had dried off, we climbed a rock and dived into the river again, splashing each other and sparring in a friendly way. Then we climbed back on to the bank we'd started from.

Through the thick vegetation we could hear the sweet call of the oriole, and above us we spotted many different varieties of birds migrating north. Matteo disappeared for a few minutes, then returned with some green leaves in his hands. "Want to smoke?" he asked. "I planted it here a while ago, I never imagined it would grow this well." His eyes sparkled with delight.

He took out some paper and rolled a long, thin joint, then lit it and handed it over to me. While we passed it back and forth we talked about our lives and our dreams, like any other teenagers would have done in any other corner of the planet. Matteo's family situation wasn't enviable. His father had died years before, and he lived alone with his mother. His older brother was wanted for questioning by the police about his contacts with the left-wing terrorist group *Brigate Rosse*—the

Red Brigade—and was hiding in some faraway country. Just like me, Matteo wasn't doing well in school; actually he wasn't doing at all, since it was three months since he'd last shown up.

"What really interests me is the piano," he explained, his emerald eyes coming alive. "I think I've got the talent." He closed his eyes and started moving his fingers through the air, as though playing on an imaginary keyboard. His head swayed gently toward his shoulders, following the tune in his head. He was so rapt in his imaginary performance that he even failed to notice when a big horsefly landed on his knee and started sucking his blood.

I realized it was getting late, and while I didn't want to interrupt Matteo in his trance, I felt a sudden rush of guilt that I had skipped school. But on reflection I decided it had been worth it, as I had made a very interesting friend and discovered an enchanting new spot to hang out during the summer.

We rode back to Siena; I hopped on the bus back home and pretended that nothing had happened. My mother noticed that I was more suntanned than I had been that morning, but as I was studying agriculture it was easy to pretend I'd had a lesson in the fields. I went to my father's office and called a classmate to find out what I'd missed. From the open window an intense scent of wisteria wafted in. The chestnuts and oaks were now full of leaves, and their perfume mingled with the sweet aroma of the acacia flowers.

A few evenings later, I was doing some homework in my room when I heard the doorbell ring. I was quite surprised when my mother called up to tell me I had a visitor. As I went down the stairs, I was even more surprised to find Matteo on the threshold chatting with my mother. He was very polite and sure of himself, and I could see that my mother was impressed. He had even brought her a bunch of wildflowers.

After I greeted him, he asked my mother if I could accompany him to his grandmother's house; it was, he said, close to our village, and we would be back for dinner. My mother consented. I got on the back of his Vespa, and this time he started off very slowly. As soon as we were a few hundred yards away, he accelerated. I gripped the seat in anticipation. Despite the tremendous velocity, he took the curves with great skill, as confident as a hawk diving toward its prey, as elegantly as the stroke of the brush. He downshifted at the entrance of each bend and accelerated at the tail end of the turn, leaning harmoniously into the curve. Minutes later he left the main road and then eased onto a long avenue lined with robust, elegant cypress trees. It ended at a large wrought-iron gate surmounted by a rusted eagle.

"This is the Castello di San Leopoldo," he said as he parked the Vespa.

"I know this is San Leopoldo! What have you in mind?" I asked.

"Absolutely nothing." He led me toward the gate.

"Do you know the owner?" I asked.

"I *am* the owner," he said with a sly grin. From his jacket he produced a ring of ancient keys, chose one, and inserted it in the bolt, then with a little gentle pressure pushed the gate open.

Before us lay the enormous medieval castle, scene of endless bloody battles, now serene in its majesty. When we got closer I could see that it was somewhat run-down and obviously no longer inhabited. The garden had run amok and some of the walls were overgrown by wild roses, which in this season were at their apex of splendor but in desperate need of trimming. Other walls were crawling with wild capers, which filled the cracks with their delicate, pale pink flowers.

Matteo headed toward the main tower, which had a beautiful mullioned window on the top floor and what seemed to be a family crest carved of marble right below it. He took out another enormous key and inserted it into the ancient bolted door.

I expected to find myself in a majestic entrance hall. Instead we found ourselves in a dark, narrow corridor; in fact we had to duck, so low was the ceiling. After a few steps Matteo opened a wooden door to his right, and we found ourselves in an expansive living room, the walls covered by tattered portraits of austere strangers.

"Ancestors," Matteo said, in a faint voice that gave me the impression he didn't want to disturb them. "That was my beloved grandmother," he added, pointing toward the painting of an elegant beauty. "She died a few years ago. We were very close. It's from her that I inherited my passion for the piano."

The center of the room was dominated by a grand piano covered by a white sheet. He flicked the sheet away with a sweeping gesture, then sat on the stool and ran his hands through his long black hair. He straightened his back and adjusted a large mirror with a carved gold-plated frame that stood next to him. He looked at his reflection for a few moments, as though seeing himself as someone entirely different. Abruptly he stood up, and from a small cupboard close to the window he produced a flask of wine and two glasses. He filled one and handed it to me, then filled his own and placed it on the piano.

He laced his fingers together and stretched them, cracking his knuckles. Then he grandly said, "The Count Matteo Saladini Becatti has the honor to perform for you Chopin's Sonata for Pianoforte."

The notes started to fill the dusty room. Matteo largely played with his eyes shut and a smile on his lips, but every now and then he would check out his position at the mirror. It seemed to me that he was extremely talented, though I was ignorant regarding the piano. I listened for more than an hour, seated on the Empire-style sofa sipping my wine. When I'd emptied my glass, I decided to explore the castle. I opened the doors, and had the impression that by doing so I would diffuse Matteo's music through hallways that hadn't seen light for God knows how long. Most of the rooms I explored were bare, but with Matteo's cascading sound track they gained an eerie fascination.

The ambience was indeed decadent, but the swirls of aromatic dust and the timeless solidity of the ancient hardwood furniture put me at ease.

I returned to the living room and sat back down on the sofa. Minutes later Matteo stopped playing. He delicately covered the piano again with the white cloth and quietly ushered me back outside.

"It's such a shame," he said as we walked back toward the Vespa. "Everyone in my family is quarreling, and meanwhile that the castle is falling apart. See the top floor?" He turned and pointed. "Half belongs to a cousin and the other half to an aunt. The second floor is divided among three other relatives, while the first is half mine and half my mother's. Ah!" He sighed. "You should have seen what a paradise it was when my grandma was alive. Now it's not even inhabitable, and the roof is leaking. She's probably turning in her grave in disgust. My family lived here for more than 600 years!" he concluded wistfully.

Minutes later he dropped me in front of my house and asked if we could meet on Saturday.

That night in bed I wondered which was the real Matteo: the

practical joker with whom I'd spent the day at the river, or the melancholy fallen aristocrat I'd encountered tonight. I fell asleep with strains of Chopin echoing in my head.

The following Saturday, Matteo invited me to lunch at his house in Siena. He lived on the outskirts of town in a rather nondescript apartment building. I took the elevator to the fourth floor and rang the bell. A tiny Filipino maid opened the door; standing behind her was Matteo, wearing his usual big grin.

He welcomed me in and introduced me to his mother, the Countess Maria Pia Saladini Becatti, a rather elderly woman who had obviously had Matteo late in life. Her hair was styled very short with interesting purplish reflections, and she wore very light makeup. She was in an elegant pea-green women's suit with a distinguished silver pin on her small pocket. The only notes of resemblance to her son were her eyes, which she highlighted with a green eye shadow. Altogether her look was rather austere, but when she shook my hand she smiled genuinely and invited me to sit next to her at the table.

She asked me many questions during the lunch, which was served by the maid and consisted of a simple plate of penne pasta and some grilled chicken breast with salad. She asked if I had a girlfriend, or if I was like her son, who was, in her words, "worse than a river that continuously changes beds." She smiled teasingly as she said it, and Matteo gave me a wink. "Just today Paola, Katia, and Lucia have already phoned," she added, "and it's not even two o'clock."

She was, I could tell, a bit concerned about her son, but was visibly proud of his studies at the music conservatory, even though she knew it would be difficult to make his passion into a profession, and she personally thought it would be wise for him to finish high school and then go to college.

When coffee was served I was shocked to see Matteo roll a joint at the table and light it. At some point the countessrealized what he was doing and spoke sharply to him: "Matteo, your behavior is utterly barbaric, stop that immediately!" But to my amazement she went on, "I've told you time and time again not to smoke pot in the dining room. Go on the terrace and wait for me!"

After their smoke Matteo asked his mother if we might go out for a walk. She consented, but made Matteo promise to return by five. He crossed his heart, kissed her on the cheek, and led me out into the streets.

The air was full of pollen, and the bees were busy about the geraniums that filled the terra-cotta pots on the windowsills of the apartment buildings. Matteo handed me the bunch of keys and said, "Today, you drive. Take me to one of *your* favorite places." I told him that we would never be back by five; he would have to break his promise. "Don't worry about my mum," he said. "I can handle her. Let's go!"

I drove the Vespa slowly—I didn't have Matteo's instinct for it. We left the city and headed north, toward my beloved Chianti hills. We passed through a vast wheat field and from the backseat Matteo started singing aloud the song "*Pensieri e Parole*" by the contemporary pop singer Lucio Battisti:

Che sai di un bambino che rubava
e soltanto nel buio giocava
e del sole che trafigge i solai, che ne sai?
E di un mondo tutto chiuso in una via
e di un cinema di periferia
che ne sai della nostra ferrovia, che ne sai?

What do you know about a child that was stealing

and only played in the dark
and about the sun that breaks through the attics,
what do you know?
And about a world closed in a street
or a cinema on the outskirts of town
What do you know about our railway, what do you
know? . . .

We continued singing for another 15 miles of twists and turns. Then I swerved onto a gravel road, raising clouds of dust that testified to the long dry spell we were going through that year. The sunlight filtered through the branches of the acacia and lime trees, illuminating the countless motes of dust that spiraled back to the ground, creating an enchanting visual effect. But we were driving without crash helmets or sunglasses, so the dust irritated our eyes and whitened our long hair. The bushes and the vegetation along the road were equally coated. Idly, I wished for a cleansing summer rainfall.

I parked the scooter on the border of a thick oak forest and told Matteo to follow me. Minutes later we came upon a clearing. I put my hands on the lower branch of a large tree and pulled myself up, then threw down a rope ladder that was tied to the trunk, and told Matteo to climb after me. After that, some metal steps had been fixed with nails and led to the top of the tree, where a solid platform made of wooden planks had been secured to the trunk with a support made of metal tubes. I had found this place by chance the previous autumn while searching for chestnuts. It had been built by some hunters to shoot squabs and then abandoned. I had modified it by taking down the first row of steps, to hide it from passersby. Now only I knew of it; it was mine alone.

The view was breathtaking, encompassing the entire Val d'Elsa and beyond. It was a strange, giddy sensation to be surrounded by treetops. The vegetation was at the height of its splendor, and the cicadas were now almost deafening.

Here and there we spotted abandoned farmhouses. Eventually my eye fell upon a stone wall at the bottom of the hill, which for some reason I had missed until then. I pointed it out to Matteo. We agreed that it looked like an abandoned mill; surely there must be some path that led to it.

"Shall we go and find out?" I ventured. Matteo nodded enthusiastically, and we scrambled down the old trunk and made our way through the thick forest.

As we pushed through the brush we heard voices, which grew progressively louder. Almost instinctively we ducked beneath a blackberry bush and waited there in silence. Soon I spotted two men in military jackets, and recognized them immediately. They were regulars at the local Communist bar who were always boasting that they were unbeatable at finding mushrooms. One of them, called Palle (Balls), summoned his friend Pampocchio and said, "I'm tired of hauling around this basket. Why not stash it here in the bushes and collect it on our way back?"

Pampocchio, the more loquacious of the two, said, "All right, Palle, do want you want. But God help you if it's not here when we come back for it. It's not the season for mushrooms, and I'll personally blame you if you lose this hard-earned batch. My mouth is already watering when I think of the sauce my wife will make with them."

"Relax. Who would ever think to look for them under this pile of leaves?" With that he buried the wicker basket, and the two continued on their way.

When we could no longer hear their voices we leapt out of hiding, tossed aside the leaves, grabbed the basket, and headed in the opposite direction toward the old mill. Matteo and I laughed merrily as we imitated the mushroom hunters' thick Tuscan accents. We tried to imagine Palle's defeated expression when he saw that his hiding place had been raided, and we kept repeating his phrase, "Who would ever think to look for them here?"

"That'll teach them to be so boastful about their escapades," I said.

When we were safely some distance away, we opened the basket and found six healthy-looking porcini mushrooms, some wild strawberries, and some fresh herbs. We decided to share the windfall; Matteo said, "This should be enough to get my mother to forgive me for being home late. She loves mushrooms!"

We were now close to the structure we had spotted from the top of the oak tree, and as we had suspected it was indeed an old mill, perched on a slow-running creek. At a first glance it was still strong and sturdy, the roof intact. We climbed the stone stairs and entered. All the furniture had been taken away, the windows were empty of glass, and the floor was full of bat and owl droppings, but the old fireplace seemed still functional.

We continued exploring, and found the enormous granite millstones still in place. We wondered how long they had rested immobile since their heyday grinding wheat into flour.

We noticed also that there were quite a number of scorpions and huge sticky webs housing alarmingly large black spiders. Even so, Matteo and I just needed a glance to realize that we had both come to the same conclusion: The old mill would be our summer getaway. We immediately started making plans, which mainly involved bringing down lots of girls and throwing some great parties; but then we decided that it would be better if it remained our private turf.

We climbed back up the hill, taking care not to bump into Palle and Pampocchio. When we reached the Vespa, Matteo decided to drive. We reached his house at 8:30 P.M., and despite his having broken his promise, Matteo's mother said absolutely nothing, and in fact thanked us for the mushrooms.

We passed many of the next free days we had cleaning the mill and trying to make it livable. We swept the floors, removed the cobwebs, and brought supplies, including candles that we placed strategically to light the place after dark. We filled some sacks with hay to be used to sleep on when we camped out at the mill.

We managed to dig up some information in the village about the mill. It had a name, *il Molin del Lupo*—the Wolf's Mill—and had been abandoned for more than thirty years. Nobody knew who the current owner was.

The original road was now overrun by brambles. We preferred to keep it that way and approached it instead by walking through the woods—even if this meant carrying heavy loads on our backs for several miles. Often we stayed overnight. Matteo brought an old battery-powered cassette player, and we would listen to entire symphonies while lying on our backs looking up at the stars. When the sun set, storms of bats would fill the sky with the nervous beating of their wings, and during the night the gloomy hoot of the barn owl would keep us awake.

Eventually Matteo's mother forced him to get a job. He went to work for a major distributor of wine and spirits, and for awhile I didn't hear from him. Even though our friendship was still somewhat young, it seemed the end of an era. Then one morning he phoned me quite early and asked me to meet him at the mill. When I got there I was surprised to see him seated before the fire on one of the rudimentary benches we had cobbled together, roasting some sausages on the embers. He passed me a bottle of wine and told me that he had been fired.

"Fired?" I said. "So soon? How did you manage it?"

He told me he had hidden a six-box carton of cheap white wine. "You know, the terrible stuff with the screw cap?" he added. "Well, when there wasn't much to do I'd take a little swig from the box. Of course, the more I drank, the more frequently I had to relieve myself. And since the bathroom was on the other side of the warehouse, I just hid behind a pallet and peed in one of the empty bottles, which I then replaced in the carton.

"Now," he continued, "can you believe my luck, one day they had a big supermarket buyer come in for a wine tasting. And the foreman, who was given the list of sample bottles to collect, finds my carton, pulls out one of the bottles I'd used as a urinal, and takes it to the tasting room."

"Matteo," I gasped, "don't tell me that they drank it!"

He looked at me as if to say *You bet they did,* and we laughed until tears were rolling down our cheeks. We kept the hilarity going by reenacting the scene of the self-important wine expert fussily going through the entire ceremony, and his expression when he took a mouthful of Matteo's vintage production.

Later that day the heat grew oppressive, and we lay on the riverbank just as we had the day we met—only a few months earlier, but it seemed a lifetime ago. Our friendship was now an essential part of our lives, and we kept in touch daily by phone as teens do. Often I would tell my parents that I was sleeping at Matteo's house and he would tell his mother he'd be staying at mine, and then we would spend the night at the mill, simply basking in the wonderful anonymity of nature and talking deep into the night, listening to the nightingales and watching in fascination the swarms of fireflies that lit up the valleys. Often in the morning we would find traces of wild boars that had wandered close while digging for roots and eating the berries on the bushes along the creek.

The mill wasn't our only refuge. We also spent many days at Matteo's castle, as he needed to practice his piano. I would listen to the wonderful sounds he conjured up with his nimble hands while I explored new rooms. Once, in the wing where his grandmother had lived, I had the eerie sensation that time had come to a standstill the day she left. The transparent Murano glass vases were filled with withered flowers and yellow stagnant water, the ashtrays heaped with white filter cigarette butts, the wardrobe piled with elegant women's clothing. Somehow the presence of the old woman in that empty, melancholy castle was still utterly vital.

One day while I listened to Matteo's treasured recording of legendary pianist Arturo Benedetti Michelangeli playing Chopin's immortal nocturnes, he produced an envelope and excitedly handed it to me. I read that he had been granted a concert performance at the prestigious Accademia Musicale Chigiana in Siena. I was so happy for him, and his eyes seemed greener than ever while I handed the letter back to him.

To celebrate he brought out two bottles of Chianti Classico Riserva. "I found them at an *enoteca*," he said excitedly. "I never saw this label before. It's called Chianti Classico Matteo, like me!" We drank the precious nectar outdoors while seated on a rock, our feet in the water and the sun in our eyes.

On the other side of the bank, hidden by a bush, Matteo spotted a small cave that had been dug out of the sandy hill. He jumped in the water, holding the second bottle of Chianti Classico aloft, and waded across, then entered the grotto and after a few minutes returned empty handed. "I hid the bottle inside. It's a perfect temperature to preserve it," he called over to me. "We'll open it after the concert, if it's successful."

"We will open it very soon I'm sure," I said as he waded back toward me. And this wasn't just rhetoric; I was certain indeed it was the case—even surer, when I saw Matteo's eyes gleaming with hope.

Shortly afterwards while holed up in my room one evening reading Jack Kerouac's *On the Road* and listening to Dylan's immortal *Blonde on Blonde*, I was interrupted by my mother's knock on the door. She told me that the Countess Saladini Becatti was on the phone.

I fell a chill of premonition as I picked up the receiver. The countess sounded alarmed and upset; in a trembling voice, she told me that her son had had an accident and suffered several fractures as well as a severe head trauma. He was out of danger for now and had asked to see me. I rushed to the garage, pulled out my own little Vespa, and tore out into the night.

I entered the medieval structure that had been serving as our hospital for 800 years, its walls and ceilings still covered in thirteenth-century frescoes. The smell of disinfectant filled my nostrils as I dashed through the corridors looking for Matteo's room. When I found it, his mother embraced me. She told me he had broken three ribs and his right arm and wrist and that three fingers had been crushed under the weight of his scooter; and there was the possibility that they might need to be amputated.

He had been highly medicated, and I was only allowed to see him through the small opening on the door. His eyes were closed but his face was a mask of pain, and his head swathed in bandages. I observed him for a few endless minutes, hoping that he was playing one of his tasteless jokes on me. Finally I tore away my gaze, kissed his mother good-bye, and returned home.

Matteo's rehabilitation was long and painful. I spent many days in the hospital with him, trying to help him through it. Fortunately his fingers were saved, but he couldn't move his wrist. Worse, he stopped smiling—I almost didn't recognize him without his ever-present grin—and when at last he was sent home he would spend hours starring at his piano in grim silence. His eyes had lost their sparkle, and he even refused to listen to music. Despite the love and care of his mother and me, Matteo seemed to retreat increasingly into a dark inner world.

He didn't react visibly when two months later the doctors confirmed that his wrist would never again become fully functional. Later he was found dead in his mother's garage, seated in her car. He had attached the exhaust pipe to a rubber hose, passed it through the window, sealed with tape any possible opening, then turned on the engine and suffocated himself.

He was found with an empty bottle of grappa, which he had apparently drunk while listening to Liszt's Ballata Number 2 in B Minor performed by Arturo Benedetti Michelangeli, playing in the cassette player as his life ebbed away.

I was dumbstruck. I locked myself in my room, refusing to see anyone for days. I couldn't even summon up the courage to attend his funeral. Eventually, though, I decided that life had to continue, and I slowly managed to put aside my grief.

In all the intervening years, there hasn't been a single day that I haven't thought about Matteo and our brief but intense friendship. Every time I hear a piano, I imagine him sitting on the rocks along the riverbed, moving his hands as if performing. Now, back on the same bank after so many years, I recall something, and beneath the carpet of stars I wade across the creek, carrying my flashlight over my head.

I enter the tiny grotto and cast my beam over the walls, till it reflects off the bottom of the bottle Matteo partially buried in the sand so many years ago. Delicately I pull it out. The label is illegible.

I take it into the mill, and there, surrounded by memories, I pull out the cork, which is completely saturated. But judging by the aroma the wine hasn't corked or gone vinegary; it smells smooth and fruity. The sediment is very high, so I delicately decant it into my wine glass and take the first sip. After over twenty years it is still more than drinkable.

I raise the glass to the skies and drink in honor of my friend Matteo. The creek is running softly; I feel alone and happy to be back in my hills.

Midnight

The stars are glittering now—my familiar stars, the constellations I've seen since childhood. I'm back outside now, laying on the grass on my back, wrapped in my sleeping bag, observing them, reorienting myself beneath them like one of the ancients.

The sky seems to whirl above me; possibly this has something to do with the nearly empty bottle at my side. And not just that bottle alone. I pause to tote up the celebratory drinks I've downed today: a few glasses with Rosanna, a few more with Cesarino, the bottle that fell from the trunk of the passing car, the awful swill the *Maestro* served in his camper, the glass Paolo shoved at me in the *enoteca*.

Still, there's no sense wasting good wine. I finish off the last of Matteo's long-hidden Chianti Classico.

As I lie back, the dizziness returns. I realize it isn't due solely to the wine; there's also the fact that just yesterday I was in America and must now be suffering from jet lag. Suddenly, the idea that I was in the United States for three months seems quite incredible. Back here, among the serene hills and ancient rhythms of my homeland, the entire experience seems as though it happened to someone else.

It occurs to me that I haven't told anyone about my American adventures. I've shared a few anecdotes, certainly, but no more. If Cristina were here, I would by now have told her everything that happened; and perhaps that would make it all the more real to me.

I turn to the empty space beside me—the space where she would be resting if only she were here—and in a voice softened by exhaustion and wine, I murmur, "It really was the most *amazing* journey. You remember, it started three months ago . . ." But that's all I can manage. I succumb to the still Tuscan moonlight.

Ringraziamenti

I wish to thank Robert Rodi, without whom this book (as well as my previous volume) would never have existed. A very special *grazie di cuore* to James Swift for his incredible kindness. I thank my parents for having decided to return to Italy when I was a child and for buying a home in this paradisiacal corner of Tuscany, giving me the opportunity to fall in love with and appreciate the area in full. I thank all the people mentioned herein, simply for existing—it's their wonderful simplicity that makes them such superb protagonists. A special thanks goes to both Katie and Jonathan, who had the patience to listen to me read the chapters after I had finished writing them, though I'm sure they often had more important things to do. I thank each and every bottle of Chianti Classico and Prosecco that I drank while writing for keeping me company during the long, lonely days.

I wish to thank the inhabitants of my village—in particular Federica, for always saying "Ohi" and for spending her spare hour patiently teaching me how to dance. A special thanks to Stefano and his wife Elisa; obviously to my *Nobil Contrada del Bruco;* and to my dear friends Andrea, Luca, and Leo. I would also like to mention Agnese who is like a sister to me, Valeria

Tignini, Valentina Tracchi, Claudia, Elena, Simone K., Franco, Annalisa, Stephanie, the Gayley family, my cousin Guido, my brother Cristiano, his wife Danda, and my nephews Anastasia, Sebastiano, and Nicolas. A *grazie gigantesco* to all those wonderful people who hosted me on my long U.S. book tour and went through so much trouble organizing many memorable events, spoiling me and making me feel at home in such a distant land. I wish to thank the friendly Backroads staff leaders and my Spanish *professoressa* Jessica. I also wish to thank Laura and Jane and Mimi who believed in me, and—why not—all those who *didn't*, which gave me the urge to prove something to them . . . and to myself.

About the Author

Dario Castagno is a local *chiantigiano* as well as a proud member of the Bruco (Caterpillar) *contrada* in Siena. He lives a peaceful existence in the village of Vagliagli in Tuscany. For more than a decade he has been guiding small groups of visitors to his favorite spots in the Chianti region of Italy where all his books have been set. Too Much Tuscan Sun- A Day in Tuscany- Too Much Tuscan Wine- An Osteria in Chianti- Seven Seasons in Siena (with Robert Rodi)- The District 9 of Chianti (with Fionn McCann)- The Miracle of Belpoggio.

Today apart from writing, he entertains his guests upon request at the Dievole winery and at the hq's of hia contrada in Siena. Visit www.dariocastagno.com for more information.

La realizzazione di un libro è un'operazione complessa,
che richiede numerosi controlli su testo e immagini;
la nostra esperienza ci suggerisce che è praticamente impossibile
pubblicare un volume privo di errori.
Ringraziamo i lettori che vorranno segnalarceli
al nostro indirizzo di posta elettronica info@betti.it
Realizzazione editoriale: Betti s.r.l.
Direttore editoriale: Luca Betti

www.betti.it - info@betti.it
Siena, Italia

Finito di stampare nel mese di febbraio 2013

ISBN 978 88 7576 292 6